NORTH AMERICAN
BACKYARD
BIRDWATCHING

For All Seasons

NORTH AMERICAN
BACKYARD
BIRDWATCHING

For All Seasons

Feeding and Landscaping Techniques Guaranteed to Attract Birds You Want Year Round

Marcus H. Schneck

CRESTLINE

© 2005 by Quarry Books

All rights reserved. No part of this book may be reproduced in any form without written permission of the copyright owners. All images in this book have been reproduced with the knowledge and prior consent of the artists concerned and no responsibility is accepted by producer, publisher, or printer for any infringement of copyright or otherwise, arising from the contents of this publication. Every effort has been made to ensure that credits accurately comply with information supplied.

This edition published in 2009 by
CRESTLINE
A division of Book Sales, Inc.
276 Fifth Avenue, Suite 206
New York, NY 10001
USA

Printed with permission of and by arrangement with Quarry Books.

First published in the United States of America under the title *The All-Season Backyard Birdwatcher* by Quarry Books, a member of
Quayside Publishing Group
100 Cummings Center
Suite 406-L
Beverly, MA 01915-6101

Library of Congress Cataloging-in-Publication Data
Schneck, Marcus.
    The all-season backyard birdwatcher : feeding and landscaping techniques guaranteed to attract the birds you want year round / by Marcus H. Schneck.
        p.   cm.
    Includes bibliographical references and index.
    1. Bird attracting. 2. Bird watching. I. Title.
QL676.5.S324 2005
598'.072'34—dc22   2005010372
                                                                    CIP

ISBN 13: 978-0-7858-2568-5
ISBN 10: 0-7858-2568-1

10 9 8 7 6 5 4

Design: Laura H. Couallier, Laura Herrmann Design
Cover Images: Maslowski Productions
Illustrations by Judy Love

Printed in China
Reprinted in 2010 (twice), 2011

For my Wife, Jill Caravan,
who understands

CONTENTS

INTRODUCTION

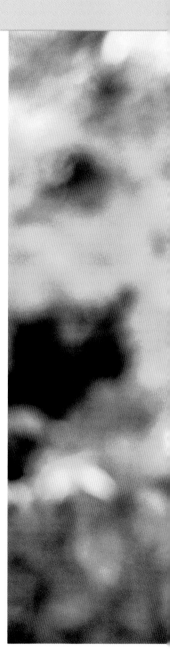

STAGES OF LIFE IN A BIRDWATCHER

Most of us were birdwatchers before we even knew that there was a name for what we were doing—let alone that there were millions of others out there doing the same thing with passion. Typically, it began with a peek into the backyard at some bright color we'd just seen flit across the landscape. Probably, there was a bird feeder out there, one that our parents had erected in our own backyard or some that the neighbors kept filled with seeds.

Putting Out Some Seed

Putting out our own seeds for the birds was the next step. Maybe we just snitched a few from our parent's larder. Maybe we gathered seeds from a plant in our garden that looked like something the birds would eat, or maybe we collected seeds from something growing wild in a neighborhood park. Maybe as part of a grade-school project, we smeared peanut butter onto a pinecone and rolled it in a pile of seed and hung it in a tree to feed the birds.

Regardless of whether the seeds we used were actually eaten by the birds, a seed of a passion was planted within us. For incredible numbers of other people across the Earth, that seed sprouts, grows, and bears fruit a bit later in life.

At this point, we're still at the early stage of bird-watching: the bird feeder stage. We plant a pole in the backyard, attach a generic feeder to the top of the pole, and pour in some seeds. Whatever birds might come by are welcomed with enthusiasm and their arrival is accompanied by feverish paging through a basic bird-identification guide. Even the squirrels that show up to raid the birdseed are greeted enthusiastically.

Bird-watching is an activity
for all ages to share together,
passing from one level of
development in skills and
knowledge to the next over
years and over a lifetime.

Backyard bird-watching is wildly popular and big business. It's estimated that a third of all American households feed wild birds, while 65 percent of residents in the United Kingdom do likewise. American statistics reveal that each bird-feeding family goes through about 75 pounds (34 kilograms) of seed each year.

Even a landscape devoid of habitat or food plants for wildlife likely will host a feeder. Even tightly manicured lawns sprout pole-topped feeders. Most birds have never been labeled "pest," which has condemned so many other creatures in the eyes of "nature-dominating" homeowners.

Part of our love affair with bird feeding is the almost-instant gratification of the activity. Planting something that would provide an ongoing, recurring source of natural food for the birds takes a season, or a few, or even longer, to begin showing results, while a feeder kept filled with seed will be visited by birds within days of its installation.

ALL-SEASON TIP

The Christmas Bird Count, which has been organized by the National Audubon Society annually since 1900, is called, justifiably, "the oldest and largest wildlife survey in the world." More than 40,000 birders take part each year, counting birds in a series of designated, circular count areas on a predetermined day near December 25, and report their counts to the Audubon Society.

Maybe the artificiality of bird feeding is the source of such strong attraction. After all, we are supplying an abnormally abundant source of food with the goal of attracting an abnormally high concentration of birds of many species. And, when it works, when the birds appear, we know it's the result of something we did "for nature."

Then, we see the same birds returning day in, day out to our feeders and we believe we are making a difference. We come to think our feeders are a necessity for those birds, rather than the supplemental food sources they really are. We start to believe that "our birds" could not survive the cold of winter without our handouts. It's not true, but it's the way we have come to think about it.

After bird-watching for awhile, you learn to identify several of the birds using your feeder on sight, maybe even to recognize the songs of a few of them. When this happens, it's time for your bird-watching credentials to jump to the next level.

Let's Try a Birdhouse

At this stage in your bird-watching life, it's time for you to put a birdhouse out there. While there are those generic birdhouses intended as one-size-fits-all, even the most basic success at encouraging birds to use a nest box—today's more generally accepted term for the birdhouse—requires a deeper level of knowledge about the birds you want to attract.

Adding the elements of providing nesting sites and caring for nestlings, such as this nest box brimming with young Carolina chickadees, to your backyard experience offers a whole new set of behaviors—different for each new species, creating opportunities for close-up observation.

Over time, the backyards of many birdwatchers become incredibly diverse habitats, packed with all sorts of plants, feeders, nest boxes, and other bird-luring devices. Brightly colored Mexican sunflowers are attractive to this female ruby throated hummingbird.

Each species has its own nesting requirements and demands from the overall size of the nest box, to the size of the entrance hole, to the height at which the nest box must be placed, to the environment into which the nest box is installed. Miss the mark by even a little on any of those key points and your chances of enticing the intended species to use your nest box fall off sharply.

Some Plants Would Help

Developing habitat (landscaping with plants that provide winter shelter; nesting sites; and edible nectar, fruits, or seeds) to attract and benefit the birds is the next step along the path to full development as a birdwatcher. Again, the level of knowledge required to make each effort pay off in additional bird visits increases. The concepts of habitat must be understood and then the specifics for the bird being targeted must be discerned and met.

Except for a few very common and very widespread species, such as sparrows and European starlings, most birds have very specific needs when it comes to what they eat, where they hide from their predators, where they find shelter from the elements, and where they hatch and fledge their young.

Many commonly used exotic (imported) species of garden and landscape plants will meet the needs of multiple species of birds. Some native plants will do even more. But, only when the relationship between a specific bird species and the plants that are native to its locale is understood, plants can be deliberately chosen to provide food, shelter, or nesting materials and sites.

Identifying "My" Birds

Eventually, those birdwatchers who continue on the path of discovery—and their numbers are growing every year—arrive at the stage of life where they want to understand the "how" and the "whys" of the birds' behaviors. Questions about identifying bird songs, migration, and social behavior take center stage. Christmas bird counts, volunteer bird surveys, and birding conferences can become part of the normal routine.

Really Understanding Birds

The book you're holding travels through all these stages of the birdwatcher's life, offering details of value at every step along the way. Whatever stage you're now occupying, you can look forward to knowing more and doing more now. Then, you can move to the next stage in short order.

1

FEEDING

Understanding Food and Feeder Preferences

We've all tried the following scenario at some point in our lives, many of us while our ages were still counted by single digits: Tear up a piece of bread or two, scatter the chunks on the ground, and wait for the birds to congregate en masse.

It should work. Bread is food, made mostly from grains and other natural ingredients. Chunks and crumbs are the right size for bird beaks, right?

Yes. English sparrows and European starlings —successful imports to North America—gather quickly, sometimes in large numbers.

But, weren't you hoping for a bright red northern cardinal, or a shimmering yellow goldfinch, or an unbelievably blue bluebird? For European feeders, the hoped-for birds might include the multicolored blue tit, sunny hued goldfinch, or brilliant green woodpecker.

We're playing much the same hopeless game (usually at ages when we should know better) when we buy the cheapest bag of birdseed we can find at the grocery store and dump it in the backyard.

Sure, the sparrows and European starlings will eat some of those seeds. But, weren't you hoping for something more colorful and interesting, something more exotic?

There's a reason you won't find generic seed mixes at wild-bird specialty stores and many home improvement stores. Producers of those cheap mixes achieve their low prices by mixing in large amounts of inexpensive materials that fill the bags but aren't attractive to most birds; materials such as milo, rice, peanut hearts, hulled oats, and wheat. Bags of just one type of select seed such as oil sunflower or thistle or premium mixes heavy in sunflower, white millet, and safflower may seem more costly in a pound-to-pound comparison, but they will be much more attractive to the bird species most of us want to attract and will result in less wasted material that the birds won't eat.

Nearly any blend with a high oil sunflower content is a premium product, and you can never go wrong by simply offering oil sunflower in nearly all your feeders. It's the single most attractive seed to the largest variety of bird species under the widest array of circumstances.

However, the other premium seeds all have their followers as well. And some species, such as the popular goldfinches, which want only niger seeds, are extremely restricted in their preferences.

Each bird species has its own seed preference (see pages 14–15). The reasons for the preferences also vary species to species, relating to the type of beak a species carries, the habitat frequented by a species, and other factors.

Emptying a bag of bargain mix on the ground will likely attract garden pests like this flock of sparrows and cottontail rabbit.

A pair of northern cardinals feast at a backyard feeder stocked with sunflower seeds, which are among their favorite foods.

Birds called crossbills are named for their scissorlike bills, which are perfectly suited to cracking open sunflower seeds.

Various bird species prefer different kinds of feeder fare. These include (left to right, top to bottom) safflower seeds, milo, striped sunflower seeds, niger seeds, oil sunflower seeds, a seed blend for finches, millet, and corn.

Species-by-Species Seed Preferences

OIL SUNFLOWER

Favorite choice for the North American feeder: black-headed grosbeak, northern cardinal, chickadees, evening grosbeak, house finch, purple finch, white-breasted nuthatch, white-crowned sparrow, white-throated sparrow. **Also attracts:** acorn woodpecker, blue jay, dark-eyed junco, downy woodpecker, gold-finches, grackle, hairy woodpecker, house sparrow, Lewis's woodpecker, mourning dove, pine siskin, red-bellied woodpecker, red-headed woodpecker, redpoll, red-winged blackbird, song sparrow, Steller's jay, tufted titmouse. **For the European feeder:** buntings, doves, dunnocks, finches, nuthatches, pigeons, siskins, sparrows, starlings, tits, woodpeckers.

STRIPED SUNFLOWER

Favorite choice for the North American feeder: blue jay, red-bellied woodpecker, Steller's jay, tufted titmouse. **Also attracts:** northern cardinal, chickadees, evening grosbeak, grackle, house finch, house sparrow, purple finch, white-breasted nuthatch, white-throated sparrow, white-crowned sparrow. **For the European feeder:** buntings, doves, dunnocks, finches, nuthatches, pigeons, siskins, sparrows, starlings, tits, woodpeckers.

SUNFLOWER HEARTS

Favorite choice for the North American feeder: pine siskin. **Also attracts:** brown-headed cowbird, northern cardinal, chickadees, goldfinches, grackle, house finch, house sparrow, mourning dove, red-winged blackbird, white-throated sparrow, wrens. **For the European feeder:** dunnocks.

SAFFLOWER

Favorite choice for the North American feeder: northern cardinal. **Also attracts:** blue jay, chickadees, house finch, house sparrow, mourning dove, red-bellied woodpecker, Steller's jay, tufted titmouse, white-breasted nuthatch.

NIGER SEED (also known as thistle seed)

Favorite choice for the North American feeder: goldfinches, pine siskin. **Also attracts:** house finch, house sparrow, mourning dove, purple finch, dark-eyed junco, song sparrow, white-throated sparrow. **For the European feeder:** finches, siskins.

CRACKED CORN

Favorite choice for the North American feeder: mourning dove. **Also attracts:** blue jay, Brewer's blackbird, brown thrasher, northern cardinal, dark-eyed junco, eastern bluebird, grackle, house sparrow, red-bellied woodpecker, red-winged blackbird, rock dove (pigeon), starling, towhee, tree sparrow, white-throated sparrow, yellow-headed blackbird. **For the European feeder:** doves, dunnocks, pigeons, sparrows, starlings.

WHITE MILLET

Favorite choice for the North American feeder: brown-headed cowbird, house sparrow, slate-colored junco, song sparrow, starling, tree sparrow. **Also attracts:** northern cardinal, chipping sparrow, pine siskin, red-winged blackbird, tree sparrow, white-crowned sparrow, white-throated sparrow. **For the European feeder:** doves, sparrows, European starlings.

SHELLED PEANUTS

Favorite choice for the North American feeder: Steller's jay, tufted titmouse. **Also attracts:** blue jay, chickadees, downy woodpecker, hairy woodpecker, house sparrow, red-bellied woodpecker, white-breasted nuthatch. **For the European feeder:** buntings, nuthatches, woodpeckers.

PEANUTS IN THE SHELL

Favorite choice for the North American feeder: blue jay. **Also attracts:** Steller's jay, tufted titmouse, woodpeckers.

Blue jays appreciate peanuts in the shell.

Beaks by Design

Beak design is the most telling bird factor. Adaptive evolution has supplied birds with a wide array of food-gathering tools to fit the various niches of the ecosystem where they originated. Some obviously do not possess the beaks of feeder-oriented species.

 SPARROW Short, thick, conical beaks, such as those of finches and sparrows, are designed for cracking open seeds and extracting the kernels inside the hulls.

 WARBLER Thin, slender, pointed beaks, such as those carried by warblers, are used to pluck insects from twigs, bark, and leaves and from among plant litter on the ground.

 **WOODPECKER** Long, heavy, chisel-like beaks—the tool of woodpeckers—are built for drilling holes into trees to get at insects that live under the bark.

 **HUMMINGBIRD** Long, delicate, tubular beaks, such as those of humming-birds, are often associated with even longer tongues and a penchant for sipping nectar from flowers.

 **CROW** Large, heavy, slightly curved, but conical beaks, such as those of crows, provide their owners with the ability to take advantage of a wide range of foods.

 **DUCK** Long, flat, fringed beak—the equipment of many ducks and other waterfowl—are designed for straining food from water.

HAWK Sharp, hooked beaks, such as those threatening tools carried by hawks and owls, are used to catch, kill, and rip apart live prey.

 **HERON** Long, pointed, spearlike beaks, carried by herons and king-fishers, also are designed for live prey but from a spearing and gulping-down approach.

| Niger | Millet | Stripe Sunflower |
| Safflower | Black Sunflower | Corn |

PROJECT: MAKE YOUR OWN SEED-SAMPLER TRAY

A divided tray feeder stocked with a half-dozen different seeds will allow you to observe birds' food preferences first hand. Filling your feeders accordingly will allow you to attract your favorites and discourage feeder pests.

Much of what we know about seed preferences among backyard bird species began with a landmark study in the 1970s, led by Aelred D. Geis of the U.S. Fish and Wildlife Service and conducted by an army of volunteers in California, Maine, Maryland, and Ohio.

Installing specially segmented test feeder trays in their backyards and filling the different sections with different types of seeds, the volunteers began to record which species of birds visited each section of their testing trays. Geis collected the data from hundreds of thousands of feeders, tallied and tabulated it into useful indicators, and developed bird-feeding into something much more closely approaching a science.

Although the tests were concluded long ago, individual backyard birdwatchers can still make their own test feeder trays, use them to gather data, and draw conclusions on their local bird populations. Such efforts have localized value because there is often variation in feeding preferences and behaviors from one locale to the next.

To make your own test feeder tray:

MATERIALS

One 1" × 8" (25 cm × 20.5 m) 8-foot (2.44 m)-long cedar or pine board *(do not use pressure-treated lumber, which may be toxic to birds)*

One 2" × 4" × 10' (5 cm × 10 cm × 3 m)

Thirty-four 1–1½" zinc-plated wood screws (4 cm)

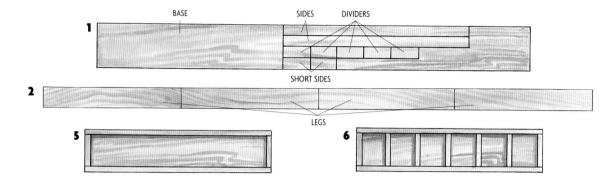

1. From the 8-foot-long (2.5 m) 1" × 8" (2.5 cm × 20.5 cm) cedar or pine board, cut one 8" × 4" (20.5 × 10 cm) base (feeder floor), two 2" × 41" (5 × 104 cm)-long sides, two 2" × 6" (5 × 15 cm)-long short sides and five 2" × 6" (5 × 15 cm)-long dividers, as shown in the illustration above.

2. Cut the 10-foot (3 m), 2" × 4" (5 × 10 cm) into four equal lengths, as shown.

3. When all the pieces are cut, take each of the two long, narrow pieces of 2" × 4" (5 × 10 cm). Position one of them along one of the long edges of the feeder base (that was cut from the 1" × 8" (2.5 × 20.5 cm), with the outside edge of the narrow (2" [5 cm]) side lined up with the edge of the feeder base, as shown in the diagram above. Screw four evenly spaced wood screws through the base into the pieces of 2" × 4" (5 × 10 cm) to attach each. Repeat with the other long, narrow piece of 2" × 4" (5 × 10 cm).

4. To create a frame around the base, attach the two short sides of the 2" × 6" (5 × 15 cm) along the short edges of the base, placing them, one at a time, atop the base with the outside of each short side lined up with the edge of the base, and screw two evenly spaced wood screws through the base to attach each side.

5. At the corners of the tray where the sides meet, attach the short sides of the tray to the long sides, by screwing one wood screw through each long side into each of the short sides.

6. Space the five dividers evenly along the inside of the frame you just created, placing the 2" (5 cm) side of each divider perpendicular from the base (as shown in the illustration of the finished feeder). Mark the positions on the bottom of the feeder and remove the dividers.

7. One by one, put the dividers into place, and attach them to the base and the long sides of the feeder by screwing two evenly spaced wood screws through the base into the bottom of each divider. Then screw one wood screw through the long side into both ends of each divider, centering the screw in the ends of the dividers.

8. Set each of the four 2" × 4" (5 × 10 cm) legs under the base, aligning one at each corner of the base (as shown in the illustration of the finished feeder). To attach the legs, screw two evenly spaced wood screws through the base, from the inside of the feeder, down into the top of each leg.

Your test feeder tray is now ready to use. (Note: If you live in a wet climate, you may want to cover your feeder with a simple plywood roof to keep the seeds dry.) Empty all your other feeders while you are running this test. Position the feeder tray in the feeder area of your backyard, and fill each section with a different type of seed. Keep a notebook handy for recording the type of seed in each section on a chart, or as a list, and noting which bird species visits each section. In about a month's time, you should know the feeding preferences of your backyard birds. You can now fill your other feeders with the seeds that will attract the birds you most desire to your backyard. While this test can be conducted any time of the year, you may attract a wider range of species if you set the tray out in spring or fall during migrations.

A snowy deck is brightened by a flock of rosy finches eagerly eating scattered seeds.

UNDERSTANDING FEEDER PREFERENCES

The right types of quality seed will increase the number and variety of birds visiting your backyard. Better yet, the right types of quality seed, offered in the right kinds of quality feeders, and in the right positions, will increase the number and variety of birds visiting your backyard by several degrees.

Combining knowledge of seed preferences with awareness of feeder types and positioning preferences, a backyard birder can even pick and choose the species of birds he wants in his backyard—within reason. (Every rule that's ever been pronounced about birds and bird feeding has just about left the lips of the rule maker by the time some bird somewhere has broken that rule. So, any rule about nature will have its exceptions.)

Some examples: Brightly colored northern cardinals like to feed near dense evergreen cover into which they can escape at the first sign of any predator. Flock-loving mourning doves appreciate a feeder on or near the ground. Goldfinches enjoy individual perches scattered along the sides of a feeding station or perches that allow them to hang upside down while feeding, as they do naturally on seed-filled flower heads.

And, the list goes on and on, demonstrating the benefit of an array of bird feeder styles hung at various heights and positions for anyone wanting to attract a large variety and large numbers of birds.

GROUND FEEDERS

Beginning at or near ground level, a simple feeding table on four legs (or atop a short pole), a large flat rock, or even a cleared area on the ground is attractive to birds that like to feed in groups, such as doves, sparrows, and the various species that are commonly called blackbirds. A quality mix of sunflower seeds, cracked corn, millet, and peanut bits will serve the widest variety of species in this situation.

The critical element for ground feeders is the elimination of any cat-concealing cover within 12 feet (3.5 m) of the feeding area. But, it should include a cluster of trees or shrubs just outside that radius to provide escape cover for the feathery diners if they feel threatened.

Bird species most attracted to this ground-feeding type of arrangement are blackbirds, brown-headed cowbird, brown thrasher, northern cardinal, chickadees, common flicker, crows, dark-eyed junco, European starling, grackles, house finch, jays, mourning dove, pheasants, quails, rock dove (pigeon), sparrows, towhees, titmice, and wood thrush.

HOPPER FEEDERS

A hopper, or house-shaped feeder is basically a feeder platform topped by a seed-dispensing bin, usually with a roof that opens for easy filling. It's generally used in an elevated position, most often at near-eye level to accommodate filling and viewing.

Most species of birds will use this type of feeder. Although smaller ones, like finches and sparrows, will dominate if the feeder is hung from a support, while larger birds, like jays, will join them regularly if the feeder is made more stable by mounting it on a pole or post.

Birds species most attracted to the hopper feeder are blackbirds, northern cardinal, chickadees, common flicker, finches, grackles, jays, mourning dove, nuthatches, sparrows, and woodpeckers.

A house-shaped feeder, also called a hopper feeder, will attract many interesting species of birds, such as this female northern cardinal and goldfinch, winter favorites across most of North America.

TUBE FEEDERS

Tube feeders are hollow cylinders of clear plastic or metal with multiple feeding ports and perches spaced along the sides. Multiple tubes are sometimes affixed into one feeder, offering increased capacity and the potential for offering multiple kinds of seeds. Perches on feeders are often short to accommodate only smaller birds. Some models include longer perches and, thus, are attractive to a wider range of species.

Tube feeders are almost always hung from a hook at the top of the tube. The most weather-proof models include a cover, several inches larger in diameter than the tube, and shaped like an inverted bowl to deflect rain, snow, and ice.

Birds species most attracted to tube feeders are northern cardinal, chickadees, common flicker, finches, goldfinch, nuthatches, titmice, and woodpeckers.

A specialized version of the tube feeder is the niger, or thistle, feeder, which has very small feeder ports designed to dispense one tiny, expensive niger seed at a time with small perches to ward off larger species. An even more specialized version of the niger feeder is the goldfinch feeder, that places tiny ports under tiny perches to allow feeding only by goldfinch. Goldfinches have evolved to eat upside-down by hanging on seed-filled flower heads.

SUET FEEDERS

The suet feeder is a wire or mesh cage or mesh bag that hangs or is mounted to the side of a house feeder, the side of a pole, or the trunk of a tree. It dispenses a beakful of suet to birds that cling to the side of the cage or bag while feeding. A crevice in the side of a tree or a hole drilled or carved into a log or branch also can serve as this type of feeder by simply pressing suet into the opening. It comes as a surprise to many that suet can be offered year round. While it's true that raw beef fat or once-rendered suet will spoil when temperatures climb above 50°F (10°C), twice-rendered suet, which is heated over a low heat to a liquid form, allowed to cool and solidify, and then done a second time, can be used safely at temperatures around 70°F (21°C).

Suet feeders, particularly those made from holes in trees, logs, or branches, are easily converted into peanut butter feeders by smearing the nutty treat into the hole instead of suet. Most of the same bird species will be attracted to peanut butter.

Birds species most attracted to suet feeders are chickadees, common flicker, jays, mockingbird, orioles, red-winged blackbird, song sparrow, titmice, white-breasted nuthatch, and woodpeckers.

PEANUT FEEDERS

Another specialized feeder is the peanut feeder, which is a wire cage with openings larger or more numerous than those in the suet feeder. The peanut feeder is designed to dispense peanuts, shelled or in-the-shell, depending on the size of the openings. Peanuts are favored by jays and nuthatches.

HUMMINGBIRD FEEDERS

Along with goldfinch feeders, hummingbird feeders are the most specialized of the lot, both in mission and, across most of North America, in season of use. Their sole purpose is to dispense sugar water through long tubes and tiny openings to hummingbirds that usually hover in front of the openings while feeding, or in some cases, may perch while feeding.

ALL-SEASON TIP

Hummingbirds are among the earliest birds to migrate northward from South America, sometimes arriving in their summer feeding grounds before nectar plants like azaleas are in bloom. When possible, they will drink sweet tree sap from holes drilled by members of the woodpecker family, but hanging out your hummingbird feeders as winter winds down will ensure that these early arrivals are well fed.

FAR LEFT
Suet feeders typically have a wire-mesh covering to dispense one beakful of suet at a time. Woodpeckers are especially attracted to suet, and this feeder with its wooden "tail support," is designed especially for woodpeckers.

LEFT
This peanut feeder has attracted an acrobatic nuthatch, an entertainingly upside down feeder.

2

HOUSING

Understanding Nesting Preferences

There are a dozen different types of bird nests. For a nesting habitat, each requires specific combinations of plants in specific arrangements and specific kinds of nesting materials, only some of which will be adaptable to any given backyard. If you are able to provide any of the situations on the right, you will greatly expand the variety of bird species that will visit your yard, allowing you to enjoy watching them do more than eat and run. To match nest to tenant, see page 38.

Offering Nesting Materials

Increase your backyard birdwatching enjoyment by encouraging birds to build nests and rear young in your backyard. All you need to do is to gather some of their favorite nesting materials, such as dried grasses, white feathers (gleaned from old pillows or feather dusters), pet fur, short scraps of yarn or string, and clothes dryer lint. Set piles of these materials where birds can see them, or hang them in mesh bags (such as onion bags or nylon mesh laundry bags) from trees, and watch which species pluck and carry them to their nests. Barn swallows, which build domed nests from mud, will repeatedly visit a mud puddle that you create in a sunny spot in the yard, carrying away one beakful at a time (for more on offering nesting materials, see page 44).

The twelve nesting habitats include the following:

- No nest—the eggs are laid on the bare ground or in a slight depression with no nest lining.

- The nest is a scraped out depression lined with lint gathered by the bird.

- The nest is a cup of nest materials woven together on the ground.

- The nest is a domed cup of nesting materials on the ground.

- The nest is a mound of nesting material on the ground or rising out of the water.

- The nest is floating, attached to water plants.

- The nest is a burrow in the ground.

- The nest is a cavity in a tree, fencepost, or similar upright wooden object.

- The nest is a platform of sticks in a tree.

- The nest is a cup of nesting materials in a tree, lined with different nesting materials. (For example, the northern cardinal builds a nest loosely woven of twigs, leaves, bark strips, and wed stalks. It then lines that with grass and hair.

- The nest is a woven bag of nesting materials hanging from a tree limb. (The northern oriole, the most famous North American bag nester, weaves its nest from plant fibers, vines, string, and strips of bark, and then lines that with hair, grass, wool, and cotton.

- The nest is a cup made of mud.

Both the male and female of many bird species work at raising their hatchlings into nestlings and on to fledglings (feathered young learning to fly). The male northern cardinal is particularly attentive in the task.

Each species of bird has its own preferences for where it will build its nest, such as these mourning doves, which looks for a suitable location rather far above the ground in the midstory or canopy of mature trees.

Matching Nest to Tenant

In addition, different bird species show a decided preference for placing their nests in very different habitats and areas within a habitat. From a bird's perspective, there are five vertical zones to any habitat. If you landscape in "vertical layers" from the ground up, you will create an attractive, natural-looking landscape that will greatly increase the number of species that visit and stay to build nests in your yard. The vertical layers of a landscape include:

- Underground, or underwater to a minimal depth. For most of us, from a landscaping perspective, underground is about the depth of the largest root system for any perennial we plant 6" (15 cm) and underwater is the depth of a man-made fish pond, 18" (.5 m).

- Ground level, where we find ground covers, short grass species, fallen logs, rocks, and the like.

- Transition level, between the very low-growing plants and shrubs where we find taller grass species, wildflowers (and garden perennials), weeds, the upper reaches of rock piles, brush piles, and the like.

- Shrub level, which can include low-growing vines, the lower reaches of taller vines, and small shade-tolerant understory trees.

- Tree level, which for some species, can include the areas not covered by trees and open to the sky.

A few species will find everything they need to live and raise their next generation in just one of those vertical zones. Most fulfill their daily requirements through a combination of two or more of the zones. The same is true for their choice of nest locations.

Although we can develop the habitat in our backyards to one extent or another to satisfy the

While it's a myth that a mother bird will abandon her brood if she smells human scent on them, the young birds can be startled into leaving the nest prematurely by too much human contact. Resist the urge to peak inside a nest box or observe a nest too closely, which can cause the nestlings to jump out of the nest. If you do cause the young birds to jump from the nest, simply pick them up and put them back into the nest.

specific needs of any species we want to attract, that's the focus of our next chapter. For now, we're concerned with those fifty species of birds that have been reported as nesting in man-made birdhouses—these days referred to as nest boxes—or the thirty species that are regular tenants in other structures provided by humans. But, keep in mind that even though these birds will nest in boxes, we must still place the boxes in a habitat conducive to attracting them.

Location preferences among some of our common species are as follows: (To learn where these birds occur, see chapter 5, page 78.)

Open ground is attractive to the dark-eyed junco, winter wren, hermit thrush, California quail, rock dove, and killdeer.

Grassland interests the dickcissel, song sparrow, field sparrow, white-throated sparrow, white-crowned sparrow, savannah sparrow, hermit thrush, eastern bluebird, western blue-bird, brown thrasher, red-winged blackbird, eastern meadowlark, common yellowthroat, ring-necked pheasant, northern bobwhite, mallard, and Canada goose.

Species attracted to shrubs for nesting are the common redpoll, blue grosbeak, indigo bunting, song sparrow, field sparrow, painted bunting, rufous-sided towhee, bushtit, ruby-crowned kinglet, northern mockingbird, brown thrasher, gray catbird, common grackle, boat-tailed grackle, red-winged blackbird, Brewer's black-bird, white-eyed vireo, black-billed magpie, loggerhead shrike, black-chinned hummingbird, Anna's hummingbird, mourning dove, and common ground dove.

In small, deciduous trees, we're likely to find the rose-breasted grosbeak, brown towhee, house sparrow, black-capped chickadee, Carolina chickadee, Carolina wren, house wren, brown creeper, tufted titmouse, bushtit, American robin, wood thrush, brown thrasher, gray catbird, northern oriole, orchard oriole, common grackle, boat-tailed grackle, red-winged blackbird, Brewer's blackbird, European starling, cedar waxwing, black and white warbler, white-eyed vireo, red-eyed vireo, American redstart, blue jay, tree swallow, violet-green swallow, eastern kingbird, least flycatcher, loggerhead shrike, northern flicker, downy woodpecker, pileated woodpecker, red-headed woodpecker, black-chinned hummingbird, ruby-throated hummingbird, Anna's hummingbird, mourning dove, common ground dove, screech owl, and American kestrel.

Although most birds are fairly secretive about their nests, a bit of careful examination at the right time of year will reveal plenty of these special sites for observing a whole new phase of a bird's life.

Nest Box Specifications

By placing just the right size nest box, with the right size entrance hole, at just the right location, we can have reasonable expectations of attracting the species we want, if it is native to our area.

The following chart lists common backyard species and provides the specifications that have proven most effective at attracting a given species to use the nest box—from size of box and entrance hole to how far off the ground the box should be installed. Use the chart both when you're buying a ready-made nest box and when you're setting out to build your own.

SPECIES	FLOOR (inches/cm)	DEPTH (inches/cm)	ENTRANCE HOLE DIAMETER (inches/cm)	ENTRANCE ABOVE FLOOR (inches/cm)	HEIGHT FROM GROUND (feet/m)
American Kestrel	7¾" × 9¼" (20 × 23.5 cm)	16" (40.5 cm)	4" (10 cm)	11½" (29 cm)	20' to 30' (6 to 9 m)
American Robin	6" × 8" (15 × 20 cm)	8" (20 cm)	Platform, not box	Not applicable	5' to 15' (1.5 to 4.5 m)
Barn Owl	10" × 18" (25.5 × 46 cm)	15" (38 cm)	6" (15 cm)	4" (10 cm)	10' to 20' (3 to 9 m)
Barn Swallow	6" × 6" (15 × 15 cm)	6" (15 cm)	Platform, not box	Not applicable	5' to 15' (1.5 to 4.5 m)
Black-capped Chickadee	4" × 5½" (10 × 14 cm)	8" (20 cm)	1¼" (3 cm)	5½" (14 cm)	5' to 15' (1.5 to 4.5 m)
Carolina Wren	4" × 4" (10 × 10 cm)	6" to 8" (15 to 20 cm)	1½" (4 cm)	1" to 6" (2.5 to 15 cm)	5' to 10' (1.5 to 3 m)
Downy Woodpecker	4" × 4" (10 × 10 cm)	9" to 12" (23 to 30.5 cm)	1¼" (3 cm)	6" to 8" (15 to 20 cm)	5' to 20' (1.5 to 6 m)
Eastern Bluebird	4" × 5½" (10 × 14 cm)	9" (23 cm)	1½" (4 cm)	6" (15 cm)	5' (1.5 m)
European Starling	6" × 6" (15 × 15 cm)	16" to 18" (41 × 45 cm)	2" (5 cm)	14" to 16" (35.5 to 41 cm)	10' to 25' (3 to 7.5 m)
Hairy Woodpecker	6" × 6" (15 × 15 cm)	12" to 15" (30.5 to 38 cm)	1½" (4 cm)	9" to 12" (23 to 30.5 cm)	10' to 20' (3 to 6 m)
House Finch	6" × 6" (15 × 15 cm)	6" (15 cm)	2" (4 cm)	4" (10 cm)	5' to 15' (1.5 to 4.5 m)
House Wren	4" × 5½" (10 × 14 cm)	8" (20 cm)	1¼" (3 cm)	5½" (14 cm)	5' to 10' (1.5 to 3 m)
Northern Flicker	7¼" × 4½" (18.5 × 11.5 cm)	24" (61 cm)	2½" (6.5 cm)	19" (48 cm)	5' to 20' (1.5 to 6 m)
Purple Martin	6" × 6" (15 × 15 cm)	6" (15 cm)	2½" (6.5 cm)	1" (2.5 cm)	10' to 20' (3 to 6 m)
Red-headed Woodpecker	6" × 6" (15 × 15 cm)	12" (30.5 cm)	2" (5 cm)	10" (25.5 cm)	10' to 20' (3 to 6 m)
Screech Owl	7¾" × 9¼" (20 × 23.5 cm)	16" (40.5 cm)	4" (10 cm)	11½" (29 cm)	10' to 30' (3 to 9 m)
Song Sparrow	6" × 6" (15 × 15 cm)	6" (15 cm)	Platform, not box	Not applicable	5' (1.5 m)
Tree Swallow	4" × 5½" (10 × 14 cm)	9" (23 cm)	1½" (4 cm)	6" (15 cm)	5' to 10' (1.5 to 3 m)
Tufted Titmouse	4" × 5½" (10 × 14 cm)	8" (20 cm)	1¼" (3 cm)	5½" (14 cm)	5' to 15' (1.5 to 4.5 m)
White-breasted Nuthatch	4" × 5½" (10 × 14 cm)	8" (20 cm)	1¼" (3 cm)	5½" (14 cm)	5' to 20' (1.5 to 6 m)

Northern cardinals, instinctively aware that their bright color makes them a target for predators, tend to choose nest sites very close to the ground in thick cover. They are most comfortable when a conifer or two is close at hand to conceal them if a quick escape is necessary.

Those species preferring to nest in small conifers include: the northern cardinal, pine siskin, chipping sparrow, black-capped chickadee, Carolina chickadee, Carolina wren, house wren, brown creeper, tufted titmouse, American robin, golden-crowned kinglet, ruby-crowned kinglet, common grackle, European starling, yellow-rumped warbler, black and white warbler, white-eyed vireo, red-eyed vireo, American redstart, blue jay, gray jay, Steller's jay, tree swallow, least flycatcher, loggerhead shrike, mourning dove, and common ground dove.

In the larger deciduous trees, we'll find the American goldfinch, house sparrow, black-capped chickadee, white-breasted nuthatch, red-breasted nuthatch, tufted titmouse, blue-gray gnatcatcher, northern oriole, orchard oriole, common grackle, boat-tailed grackle, Brewer's blackbird, European starling, cedar waxwing, yellow-throated warbler, black and white warbler, red-eyed vireo, blue jay, American crow, tree swallow, violet-green swallow, eastern kingbird, least flycatcher, loggerhead shrike, northern flicker, downy woodpecker, pileated woodpecker, red-headed woodpecker, ruby-throated hummingbird, screech owl, American kestrel, and the red-tailed hawk.

Those species showing a preference for large conifers include the purple finch, evening grosbeak, red crossbill, black-capped chickadee, white-breasted nuthatch, red-breasted nuthatch, tufted titmouse, golden-crowned kinglet, ruby-crowned kinglet, common grackle, European starling, yellow-rumped warbler, yellow-throated warbler, black and white warbler, red-eyed vireo, blue jay, American crow, tree swallow, least flycatcher, loggerhead shrike, and red-tailed hawk.

ALL-SEASON TIP

Waiting until you notice courting behavior among the birds in your backyard before placing your nest boxes dooms your efforts to failure if you want to encourage birds to use your nest boxes. Get those nest boxes into place well before the courting and mating season. In the southern half of the United States, that means setting out nest boxes in February. In the northern United States and Canada, put out nest boxes in mid-March.

When it comes to birdhouses, beauty is in the eye of the beholder. A bird will call it home if the entrance hole is the right size. For the sake of safety, it's best for it to not have a perch, because predators can use them as a toehold when invading nests, and birds, which can land in the opening, don't need them.

Selecting Ready-Made Birdhouses

There are many wonderful nest boxes, or birdhouses, available commercially. On the other hand, there are quite a few that are ornamentally beautiful but will not serve the needs of the birds, or even worse, could become deathtraps for them.

Begin any nest box search by knowing the species of bird you would like to attract and by consulting the chart on page 40. While there are exceptions to any rule, a nest box that doesn't at least come close to the proper dimensions for the intended species has very little chance of success.

Next, the nest box must have holes or slots for drainage and ventilation. Water gathering in the bottom of a nest box can become a breeding ground for disease, or worse, collect and drown baby birds. A box that doesn't allow air to circulate through the interior runs the chance of overheating nestlings in the warmer months of the year. Sometimes, if a nest box meets all other specifications, you can use a drill to add drainage and ventilation holes.

Make sure you can easily access the interior of the nest box. A roof or side panel that hinges out or lifts away makes for easy cleaning of the box after the birds are through with it at the end of the season. It also allows easy, discrete inspection and monitoring while birds are using it.

ALL-SEASON TIP

Many insect pests in spring and summer can become a problem in nest boxes intended for birds. These range from parasites, like the blow fly, to those seeking to put the nest box to their own housing use, such as wasps. Inspect your nest boxes before nesting season, whenever a nesting attempt by a bird seems to have failed, and again after the nesting season. Remove and dispose of abandoned and infested nesting material or nests built by the insects. For extreme infestations, spray inside the nest box after removing the nest with an insecticide containing the organic active ingredients of pyrethrin or rotenone. Apply according to label instructions, and make sure that the label ensures that the product is safe for use around birds.

A nest box should be made of nontoxic materials and left unfinished or coated with nontoxic paint. After all, we're talking about a nursery for baby birds here. There should be no paint or stain whatsoever on the inside of the nest box.

It should be made of thick wood, $\frac{1}{2}$ inch (1.5 cm) or more, or other material that will provide some insulation against heat and cold for the baby birds and their parents. Because it is a poor insulator, metal is generally not a desirable material for the construction of nest boxes, except in the special case of purple martin houses, which are typically made of aluminum.

The nest box roof should extend out over the front, back, and sides, and especially out beyond the entrance hole by several inches. Like a porch roof on a house, the roof on a nest box prevents rain from getting into the nest box.

If you buy a nest box that has a perch attached outside the entrance hole, be sure to remove the perch. Cavity-nesting birds don't need perches, but predators can, and do, use them as footholds while attempting to capture and kill birds inside the nest box. Perches also help European starlings and house sparrows to make use of a nest box intended for a more interesting or rare species.

Bright colors may appeal to our aesthetic sense, but birds prefer to nest in naturally camouflaged spots that attract less attention from their predators and other animals that might interfere with their nesting attempts. To ensure that your boxes find occupants, stick with colors that are in muted earth tones, again except in the special case of purple martin houses, which are traditionally white—the preferred color of this species.

Commercial nest boxes don't come with the following apparatus preinstalled in the bottom, but we should add it to every box we deploy, whether store-bought or homemade. Form a small, $\frac{1}{2}$-inch-deep cage from chicken-cage fencing that is woven with small openings. It should fit the inside dimensions of the nest box, and be placed on the bottom of the box so that it forms a raised floor to protect nestlings from parasites, by allowing the parasites to drop through the mesh.

A relatively small nest box with a correspondingly small entrance proves to be just the right enticement for a tufted titmouse looking to build its nest for the spring, even though that nest box is located in a busy area just off this house's patio.

PROVIDING NESTING MATERIALS

Some birds, such as this grass-collecting American robin, are very precise in the materials they will incorporate into their nests. However, other species, such as grackles, will incorporate a bewildering array of materials, such as plastic bags, into their nests if they come across them when they are building.

Some birds do a lot of material gathering as they build nests, and each species has its preferences for nesting materials. Orioles and northern cardinals quickly snatch up any bit of available yarn. Chipping sparrows and song sparrows grab every strand of hair—animal or human—that they spot. Swallows love feathers, particularly white ones. Grackles will incorporate all sorts of debris into their nests including items such as plastic bread bags and balloons.

We can offer safe, favored materials to the birds in our backyards as easily as draping 6" to 8" (15 to 20-cm) strands of yarn and string over porch rails, along clotheslines, and over the branches of trees. Mesh onion bags can be stuffed with feathers (gleaned from old pillows or feather dusters), hair (a good use for pet

groomings), straw, and the like, and hung in the backyard where birds will see them. Stick with one or two bright colors, and you'll be able to easily spot your offerings in the nests the birds eventually build.

Calcium is another material eagerly sought by birds during the nesting season. To give them a calcium boost, toast chicken eggshells in the oven, (for about 30 minutes at a low setting), and when dried and cooled, crush them and offer the bits in your feeders, particularly in feeder trays where they will be easily seen. Bluebirds, finches, flickers, jays, sparrows, and orioles will make short work of the crushed-eggshell supply. Some observers have reported decreased nest predation by blue jays when eggshell calcium has been offered because that satisfies the jay's need for calcium in its diet.

Keeping Predators Out of Nesting Boxes

A nest full of eggs or baby birds is a major attraction for all sorts of predators, ranging from squirrels, raccoons, and free-roaming domestic cats to snakes and other birds. That's one of the reasons that so many bird species, through evolution, moved up into the trees for nesting in the first place.

Most nest boxes (and bird feeders too) in the backyard benefit from some sort of antipredator measures. These measures can be as simple as mounting the box on a slippery PVC or metal pole to dissuade climbing predators.

Metal or plastic disc- or funnel-shaped baffles can be used to surround the nest-box pole or tree trunk and force a predator to give up when it can't climb over the barrier. Metal baffles will stand up to attacks by the predators and the elements better than plastic.

Metal attached to the nest box, surrounding the entrance hole, will thwart predators, such as squirrels and raccoons, which might be tempted to chew around an unprotected hole, enlarging it for easier access to the birds inside.

A block of 1" (2.5 cm)-thick wood with a hole cut in the center to the same dimension as the entrance hole will thwart the attempts of predators such as cats or raccoons when they try to reach inside the nest box with a paw.

Entrance-hole diameter is critical to making sure your nest box is used by the intended species. Holes that are larger than needed are attractive to big, nuisance birds such as European starlings, house sparrows, and other nest invaders.

Baffles around the poles supporting feeders have proven more effective against predators such as cats, raccoons, and snakes than against seed-stealing squirrels that usually find their way around the baffle.

BUILD YOUR OWN BIRDHOUSES

All of the preceding considerations also apply to boxes that you make yourself. Now, here are the steps to put those dimensions into action, making a nest box that has the dimensions required by an eastern or western bluebird. (To modify this pattern to fit other bird species, substitute the entrance-hole dimensions listed in the chart on page 40 for the species you want to attract.)

PROJECT: NEST BOX

MATERIALS

One 5' (1.5 m)-long exterior grade, 1 × 6 (2.5 × 15 cm) board

Approximately 20 1³/₄" (4.5 cm) galvanized wood screws

One 1³/₄" (4.5 cm) galvanized nail

¹/₄" (0.6 cm) drill bit

1 From the board, cut all pieces as shown on the pattern, below.

2 After the pieces are cut, drill an entrance hole in the piece that will become the front of the box. Six inches (15 cm) up from the bottom of this piece, use a drill and a ¹/₂" (1.5 cm)-wide spade bit to drill a centered, 1¹/₂" (4 cm)-diameter entrance hole, as shown in the illustration of the assembled nest box.

3 Next, place a saw at a 45-degree angle, and saw off about ¹/₄" (2 cm) of each corner of the floor. Then, drill a few randomly spaced holes in the bottom to create drainage.

Note: Whenever the following instructions call for you to attach two pieces with screws, predrill the holes first to keep from splitting the wood when you insert the screws. Also, note that the back of the box is longer than all the other pieces and is intended to extend below the bottom of the nest box for stabilization and to provide extra room for mounting the box to a pole or tree with screws.

4 Attach one side piece to the back of the box with two screws. Align the edge of the side with the outside of the back. The longest edge of the side should be connected to the back with the top of the side even with the top of the back.

Make the cuts shown in the board to form the various pieces of the bluebird nest box.

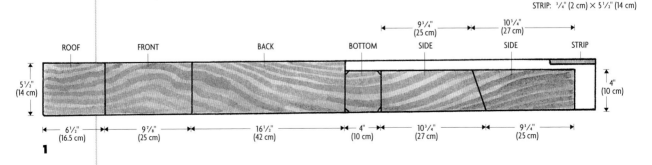

STRIP: ³/₄" (2 cm) × 5¹/₂" (14 cm)

ROOF   FRONT   BACK   BOTTOM   SIDE   SIDE   STRIP

9³/₄" (25 cm)   10³/₄" (27 cm)

5¹/₂" (14 cm)   4" (10 cm)

6¹/₂" (16.5 cm)   9⁷/₈" (25 cm)   16¹/₂" (42 cm)   4" (10 cm)   10³/₄" (27 cm)   9³/₄" (25 cm)

1

5 Attach the floor to the back and side, recessing the floor ¼" (0.5 cm) above the bottom of the side. Use two screws to attach the floor to the back and two screws to attach the flood to the side.

6 Attach the front to the floor and side, using two screws in each attachment.

Note: Steps 7 and 8 will create hinged side to the nest box, to allow easy access for cleaning out old nesting materials.

7 Attach the top only of the second side to back, with only one pivot screw through the back into the side about 2" (5 cm) down from the top as shown below.

8 Attach the second side to the front, with only one pivot screw through the front into the side about 1" (2.5 cm) down from the top as shown below.

9 Attach the roof with the back of the roof flush with the back of the back and the front of the roof extending out beyond the front. Use two screws each to attach the roof to the first side, the back and the front. Do not attach the roof to the now-hinged second side.

10 Push the second side/door closed. Drill a hole through the front into the second side/door about 1" (2.5 cm) up from the bottom. This will provide a mechanism to keep your second side/door securely closed until you want to open it.

The hinged side panel of this next box is critical to its success. Having access to clean the box will ensure many uses of the nest box as bluebirds prefer to start each new nest in a clean setting.

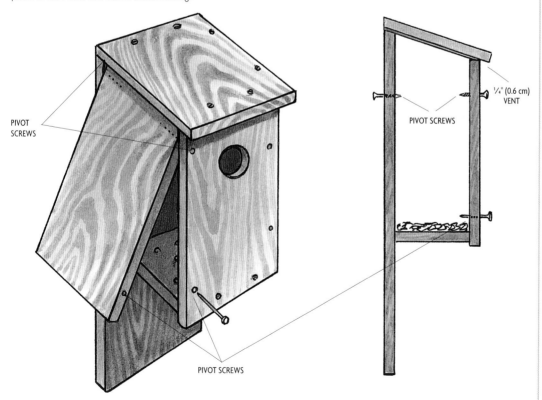

PIVOT SCREWS

PIVOT SCREWS

PIVOT SCREWS

¼" (0.6 cm) VENT

PROJECT: PLANTATION HOUSE

MATERIALS

20" (50.8 cm) square ³⁄₄" (1.9 cm) exterior grade MDF

12" (30.5 cm) square ¹⁄₄" (0.6 cm) exterior grade MDF

One 8" × 1¹⁄₈" × 1³⁄₈" (20.3 × 2.9 × 3.4 cm) softwood

One 6" × 1¹⁄₈" × 1³⁄₄" (15.2 × 3.4 × 4.4 cm) softwood

One 10" (25.4 cm) length ⁷⁄₈" (2.2 cm) hardwood dowel

Yellow glue	Brads
Sandpaper	Exterior grade paint
Try square	Jigsaw
Plane	Hammer
Backsaw	Bracing board
Awl	Chisel
Electric drill	1¹⁄₄" (3.2 cm) spade bit
Paintbrushes	Pencil

1 On the ³⁄₄" (1.9 cm) MDF lay out the base 14" × 7¹⁄₂" (35.6 × 19.1 cm), the bottom 11¹⁄₂" × 5¹⁄₈" (29.2 × 13 cm), two sides 11¹⁄₂" × 5¹⁄₈" (29.2 × 13 cm), and two ends 5¹⁄₈" × 7⁵⁄₈" (13 × 19.4 cm) of the birdhouse. (Layout the two ends so that the peak forms at a 90° angle.) Cut slightly oversize with a jigsaw and trim to lines with a plane.

2 Use a plane to chamfer three edges of the base, and sand smooth.

3 Glue and nail all these pieces together.

4 When the glue has set, trim off any irregularities with a plane.

5 Lay out and cut two piece of ¹⁄₄" (0.6 cm) MDF for the roof, trim to 4³⁄₈" × 12¹⁄₄" (11 × 31.1 cm) with a plane and then glue and nail these to the main body of the birdhouse.

6 On the ¹⁄₄" (.6 cm) MDF lay out the four small squares 1³⁄₈" × 1³⁄₈" (3.4 × 3.4 cm) for the pillar bases and tops. Cut with a backsaw and then smooth off the edges with medium grit sandpaper. Draw diagonal lines to find the center and make an indentation with an awl.

7 With a backsaw and a bracing board, cut two piece of ⁷⁄₈" (2.2 cm) dowel 4¹⁄₂" (11.4 cm) long. Then glue and nail the pillar bases to the dowel.

8 Chamfer the pillar bases and tops with a chisel.

9 From the remaining ¹⁄₄" (0.6 cm) MDF cut a piece for the door 2" × 3¹⁄₈" (5.1 x 7.9 cm) and four ³⁄₄" × 2³⁄₄" (1.9 x 7 cm) pieces for the window. Glue and nail the door into position but leave the windows.

10 From a scrap of ³⁄₄" (1.9 cm) MDF, cut a triangle 4" × 5¹⁄₈" (10.2 × 13 cm) from the top of the portico. Sand the edges; mark the middle and make a hole with the electric drill fitted with a 1¹⁄₄" (3.2 cm) spade bit. Tidy up the inside of the hole with sandpaper. Sand any marks left by the spade bit.

11 Assemble the portico by gluing and nailing.

12 Mark and cut two angled pieces of ¹⁄₄" (0.6 cm) MDF for the portico roof 3³⁄₈" × 4" (8.4 × 10.2 cm); glue and nail these into position.

13 Glue and nail windows into position.

14 From the two pieces of softwood, cut the wood for the spires; two 3¹⁄₂" (8.9 cm) long from the thinner piece and one 5" (12.7 cm) long from the thicker. Mark out 90° V-shapes on them and cut away with a backsaw, so that they sit precisely on top of the roof. With a pencil, mark in ¹⁄₄" (0.6 cm) halfway up the spires and reduce the width with the backsaw to create a stepped effect.

15 Mark lines for a pyramid point, cut with backsaw, and glue and nail these to the roof.

16 Using a medium grade grit sandpaper, remove any saw marks.

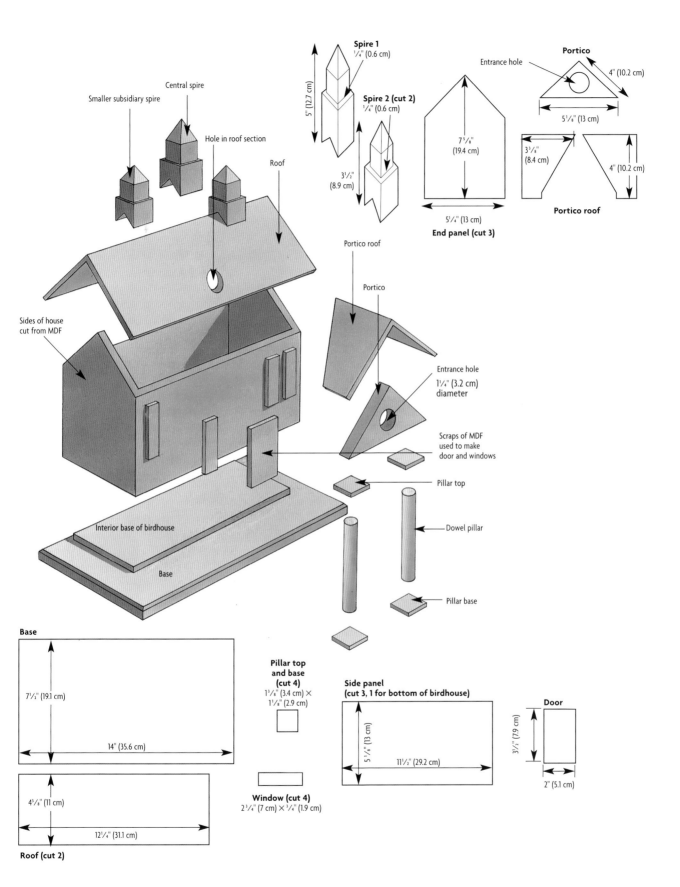

Smaller subsidiary spire

Central spire

Hole in roof section

Roof

Spire 1
$\frac{1}{4}$" (0.6 cm)

5" (12.7 cm)

Spire 2 (cut 2)
$\frac{1}{4}$" (0.6 cm)

$3\frac{1}{2}$"
(8.9 cm)

Entrance hole

Portico

4" (10.2 cm)

$5\frac{1}{8}$" (13 cm)

$7\frac{5}{8}$"
(19.4 cm)

$3\frac{3}{8}$"
(8.4 cm)

4" (10.2 cm)

Portico roof

$5\frac{1}{4}$" (13 cm)

End panel (cut 3)

Portico roof

Portico

Sides of house
cut from MDF

Entrance hole
$1\frac{1}{4}$" (3.2 cm)
diameter

Scraps of MDF
used to make
door and windows

Pillar top

Dowel pillar

Interior base of birdhouse

Base

Pillar base

Base

$7\frac{1}{2}$" (19.1 cm)

14" (35.6 cm)

**Pillar top
and base
(cut 4)**
$1\frac{3}{8}$" (3.4 cm) ×
$1\frac{1}{8}$" (2.9 cm)

**Side panel
(cut 3, 1 for bottom of birdhouse)**

$5\frac{1}{8}$" (13 cm)

$11\frac{1}{2}$" (29.2 cm)

Door

$3\frac{1}{2}$" (7.9 cm)

2" (5.1 cm)

$4\frac{3}{8}$" (11 cm)

$12\frac{1}{4}$" (31.1 cm)

Roof (cut 2)

Window (cut 4)
$2\frac{3}{4}$" (7 cm) × $\frac{3}{4}$" (1.9 cm)

Project: Prairie House

MATERIALS

Two 84" × 1" (213.4 × 2.5 cm) diameter dowel

One 12" × 3" × ¾" (25.4 × 7.6 × 1.9 cm) timber

One 14" × 30" × ½" (35.6 × 76.2 × 1.3 cm) plywood

One 9" × 3" × ¾" (22.9 × 7.6 × 1.9 cm) timber (blocks)

One 10¾" × 3" × 1" (27.3 × 7.6 × 2.5 cm) timber

One 8" × ⅜" (20.3 × 1 cm) quarter-round bead

One 18" × 14" × ½" (45.7 × 35.6 × 1.3 cm) plywood

One 13½" × ¼" (34.3 × 0.6 cm) diameter dowel

One 2" × ½" (5.1 × ⅓ cm) diameter dowel

Exterior wood glue   Stain and paint

¾" (1.9 cm) molding pins   Screws

1 The walls and roof of our log cabin are made from 1" (2.5 cm) half-round bead. Cut the two end panels from ⅜" (1 cm) plywood, scoring across the grain with a craft knife and finishing the edges square with a plane. Drill the entrance hole with a hole-saw to suit specific bird species.

2 Cut the half-round dowel into seven lengths and plane a narrow flat along each edge. Cut one piece in half lengthwise for the top rails.

3 Glue and pin the rails to the two end pieces, gluing each horizontal joint as you proceed, and check that the end panels are vertical and square to the sides. Fit the narrow pieces at the top of the wall, and when dry, plane the top edges to follow the roof angle.

4 Cut the flat center roof-ridge member to length from ⅛" (0.3 cm) plywood to finish flush with the outer face of the two end walls. Glue and pin this in place. When dry, plane the edges to match the roof angle. Cut the two roof panels to size from ⅛" (0.3 cm) plywood, finishing flush with the outer face of the end and side walls. Glue and pin in place.

5 Cut 22 lengths of half-round dowel ¼" (0.6 cm) longer than the width of the angled roof panels. Glue and pin these to the roof panels as shown, checking that no pins protrude through the underside. Carefully cut the top corner of each piece to form a flat surface on either side of the ridge board. Glue and pin a length of half-dowel flat onto the ridge board starting from the chimney.

6 Cut the chimney from a 10¼" (26 cm)-piece of 3" × 1⅛" (8.6 × 2.9 cm) wood, using a back saw to cut partway down the length and across at an angle of 45° to form the narrow section. Cut two ⅛" (0.3 cm) grooves at the top. Cut a ⅛" (0.3 cm) plywood plate slightly larger than the chimney top and glue and pin it over the grooves. Glue and screw chimney to the wall.

7 Cut four lengths of half-dowel to form the vertical corner pieces and further lengths to fit between these to cover the rear and front walls, leaving the window and door openings.

8 Cut the vertical division to fit to the underside of the roof. Cut the floor to the width of the house and glue and pin the two pieces together. Cut two 5" (12.7 cm) pieces of ¾" (1.9 cm) quarter-round bead, support battens slightly shorter than half the internal house length and glue them to the inside walls.

9 Cut the baseboard to size 14" × 18" (35.6 × 45.7 cm) from ½" (1.3 cm) plywood and round the corners. Mark out and cut the two support brackets from ¾" (1.9 cm) wood. Screw the two pieces together and position them on the underside of the base-board. Drill through the baseboard and glue and screw the battens to the underside.

10 Cut the ¾" × ¾" (1.9 x 1.9 cm) rear locating batten to the full internal width of the house. Screw this batten centrally, 1½" (3.8 cm) from the rear edge. Cut the front-locating block and drive a 1½" (3.8 cm) brass screw into the center of the front face, leaving ¾" (1.9 cm) of the shank protruding. Cut the head off the screw and file the edge smooth. To mark the hole position for the locating stud, rub a pencil point against the end of the screw to leave graphite deposits. Center the outside face of the door on the stud and push the house against the stud end. Use a drill of equal diameter to the stud to drill the locating hole, after transferring the mark to the outside face.

11 Cut the rail to length from $1/4$" (0.6 cm) diameter dowel. Cut two short lengths of $1/2$" (1.3 cm) diameter dowel (or square bead) and file a recess in one end of each to take the rail. Drill a pilot hole in the end of each post and drill and screw through the baseboard to secure them.

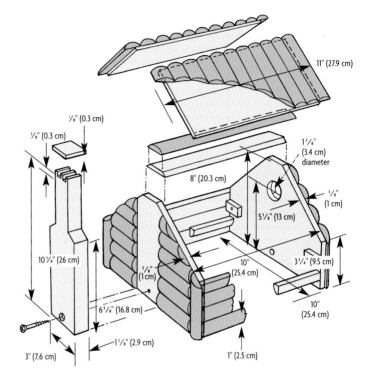

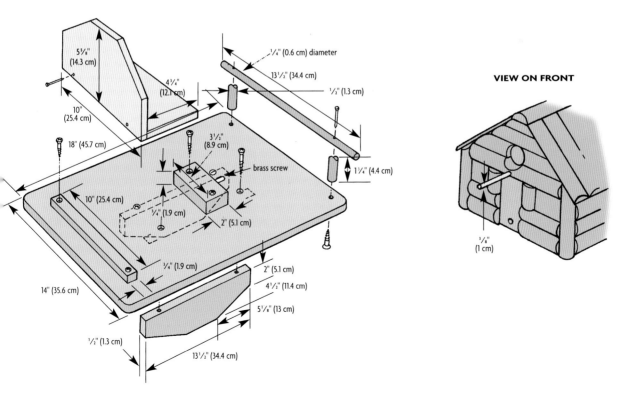

VIEW ON FRONT

PROJECT: HOLLOW LOG BOX

MATERIALS

One log 8"–14" (20.3 cm–35.6 cm) diameter

One 6" × 6" × ³/₈" or ¹/₄" (15.2 × 15.2 × 1 or 0.6 cm) plywood

One 3" × ¹/₄" (7.6 x 0.6 cm) diameter dowel

1 length of stiff wire

screws

Router and large diameter (³/₄" (1.9 cm) plus) straight bit

¹/₂" (1.3 cm) diameter flat or spade bit

1 Cut both faces of the branch or log with a saw, leaving it flat and reasonably smooth. If required, use a chisel and wooden mallet to enlarge the hole. Work with the grain direction, cutting away thin shavings. If you wish to cut a new hole in a log, use a flat bit or auger to drill a ring of holes. Knock out the center waste and pare the sides with a chisel to finish them smooth.

2 Choose a round container, paint can or similar, that is about 1" (2.5 cm) larger in diameter than the irregular hole in the log. Place this over the irregular hole and raw round it with a pencil.

3 Fit a large-diameter straight cutter in the electric router.

4 Set the depth of cut to ¹/₈" (.3 cm). With the router firmly supported on the timber face and firmly gripped in both hands, cut round the edge of the hole in a clockwise direction. Aim to

remove about ¹/₄" (0.6 cm) of wood from the edge at a time, slowly increasing the rebated area up to the line. Having cut around the line, increase the depth of cut and repeat the process until the full ¹/₂" (1.3 cm) is completely removed.

5 Alternatively, a sharp chisel can be used, first marking the depth of the hole and cutting from the side before cutting to clear the remaining wood. Use a wooden mallet to drive the chisel.

6 On ³/₈" (1 cm) plywood, draw around the contained used to mark out the rebate. Cut out the circular plate with a jigsaw and trim with a rasp until it is a fairly close fit in the rebate in the log.

7 Use a holesaw to cut the entrance hole when fitting a plate to the front of a hollow log. Drill a small hole or cut a small notch at the bottom of the plate to allow for drainage.

8 If preferred, the outside face of the plate can be painted with masonry paint or water-based stain or varnish, before being fitted. Screw or nail the plate into the rebate.

9 To enable the log to be hung on a wall or post, bend a piece of stiff wire with a circular twist at each end, and fix it to the back of the log with two wood screws.

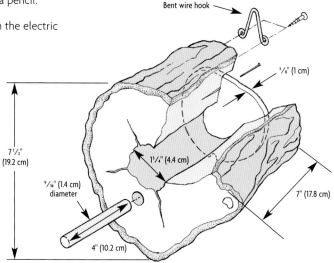

Bent wire hook

¹/₈" (1 cm)

7¹/₂" (19.2 cm)

1³/₄" (4.4 cm)

⁹/₁₆" (1.4 cm) diameter

7" (17.8 cm)

4" (10.2 cm)

Project: Clay Pot Box

MATERIALS

Terra-cotta flowerpots 6"–12" (15.2 cm – 30.5 cm) diameter

One 12" × 12" × ³⁄₈" or ¼" (30.5 × 30.5 × 1 cm or .6 cm) plywood

Screws

Terra-cotta paint

1 Using any size of traditional terra-cotta flower pot, measure the inside diameter within the stepped rim of the pot.

2 Set a pair of compasses to that diameter and draw out the circle on ³⁄₈" (1 cm) thick solid wood or plywood. Score along the line and cut around it with a jigsaw.

3 Use a masonry bit to drill two holes in opposite sides of the pot rim, and use a larger drill to countersink them.

4 Either cut an entrance hole, the size depending on the pot and the bird species you wish to attract, or cut part of the circle away to produce an open-front birdhouse. At the bottom of the disk cut a small notch across its edge to allow the pot to drain if necessary.

5 Block the drainage hole in the base of the terra-cotta pot with an epoxy filler plug.

6 Fit the disk in the rim of the pot and insert the two screws.

7 Paint the outside face of the disk with terra-cotta masonry paint.

8 Use stiff garden wire to make a cradle for hanging the pot in a tree or bush. Alternatively, cut a small-diameter wooden disk, slightly larger than the drainage hole in the end of the pot, and drill a hole through its center. Screw the pot onto a wall or wooden surface using a long wood screw and an angle block to tilt the pot downward.

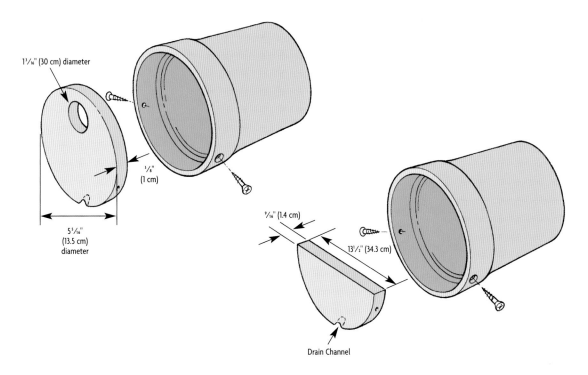

1³⁄₁₆" (30 cm) diameter

¹⁄₈" (1 cm)

5⁵⁄₁₆" (13.5 cm) diameter

⁹⁄₁₆" (1.4 cm)

13¹⁄₂" (34.3 cm)

Drain Channel

Project: Build a Birdhouse from a Gourd

ative Americans may have started the tradition of building birdhouses when they dried and hollowed out large gourds. They fashioned gourds into nest boxes to attract insect-destroying purple martins to their cultivated fields of corn, beans, and squash—their major crops.

This tradition is making a major resurgence today. Seeds for birdhouse gourds are now available in garden catalogs and in garden sections of home improvement stores. And, in addition to purple martins, a variety of other bird species will take advantage of the unique nest "box."

MATERIALS

Gourd

Spade drill bit or hole saw (sized according to species the gourd is intended for)

¼" (0.6 cm) drill bit

2' (0.6 m) piece of rawhide cord or craft-gauge wire

Household chlorine bleach

Sponge or rag

Nontoxic paint or wood preservative

1 After growing a gourd to maturity, leave it on the vine until the vine dies in the fall. Pick it, and hang it in a dark, dry location (such as an attic, closet, or garage) for several months.

2 When the gourd is bone-dry to the touch and the seeds inside rattle around, sounding like bits of paper and cardboard, it is ready to turn into a nest box. First, wipe the gourd with a rag dipped in a weak solution of household bleach and water to clean any mold from the exterior surface.

3 Cut an entrance hole in the largest-diameter section of the gourd, using a drill and a spade drill bit or hole saw sized for the species you want to attract (see chart on page 40).

4 Through the entrance hole, shake out all the dried seeds and inside matter. (The seeds can be saved in a cool, dry environment for future planting.)

5 Drill two small holes near the top of the gourd, (points **A** and **B**), using the ¼" (0.6 cm) drill bit, and drill a few drainage holes in the bottom of the gourd.

6 String a rawhide cord or wire through the holes for hanging the nest box.

7 Paint the gourd with exterior-grade, nontoxic paint, or coat it with an exterior wood protectant. When coated, it should last for several seasons.

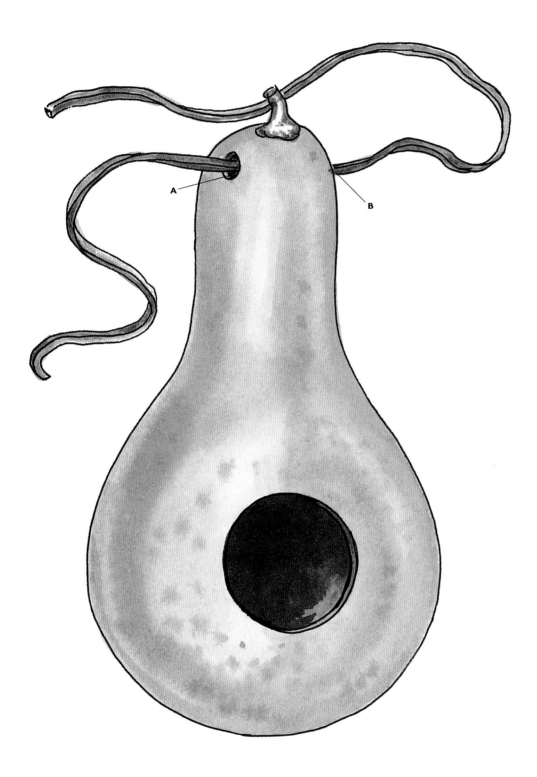

A

B

Make sure your gourd is bone-dry before attempting to cut the entrance hole. You'll be able to hear the seeds rattling around inside when you shake a gourd that is dry enough for use.

3

HABITAT

UNDERSTANDING HABITAT

There are five basic requirements of life that nearly every living creature must have in order to survive and to perpetuate its species. They are food, water, shelter from enemies and inclement weather, a safe and secure place to reproduce and rear young, and space or territory.

Most of these requirements must be met every day. Others, such as shelter from inclement weather, need to be satisfied less frequently, but when the need arises, the need for them is equally pressing.

As a group, these requirements are known as the "niche" for a species. Over thousands of years, the species and the elements of its niche have evolved together, adapting physically and behaviorally to take advantage of one another. That's why plants with bright red, tubular flowers and hummingbirds with long, strawlike bills and even longer tongues, are a perfect fit.

In the backyard, we can use our knowledge to attract any bird species native to our area.

Some Basic Landscaping Principles

Landscaping is an art form that can be practiced by anyone. Landscaping to attract wildlife is a hobby that's almost mandatory for those who would bring as wide a variety of birds as possible into their backyard.

The process consists of six basic steps:

1. Assess what plants you already have on your property.
2. Gather new ideas.
3. Create a landscape plan.
4. Remove and replace elements no longer desired.
5. Install new plants, water features, and hardscape (paths; patios; and other permanent, man-made structures).
6. Maintain the landscape.

Begin by spending some time with your existing landscape. Try to get a deeper understanding of what's already there, how it's functioning, and what it's providing for birds that you've ever attracted. Expect to be surprised. Take notes.

You may want to start with some general impressions. Use a pencil to move your thoughts onto graph paper. The small squares of graph paper are designed to allow you to draw something to scale and to keep everything in perspective.

Choose a scale and stick with it. In a small backyard, a scale of one-grid square on the graph paper representing one-square foot of

Carefully charting your backyard before beginning any major changes or additions will help you to visualize just the right spot for another nest box, a new feeder, a water feature, or whatever you have in mind.

The rufous-sided towhee chooses a heavily vegetated spot on or near the ground where its natural camouflage is most effective to build its nest of leaves, bark, weeds, and stems.

your property might work just fine. On a larger property, each grid square will need to represent much larger on-site spaces, unless you use several pieces of graph paper taped together.

Measure the area you want to work on, and review the elements already there. Feel free to work to such detail as using a surveyor's tape measure or as loosely as pacing off the distances.

After getting the rough overall dimensions of the area down on paper, outline every structure that currently exists on the property: the house,

other buildings, deck, patio, driveway, sidewalk, swimming pool, and other man-made elements. Simple squares, rectangles, circles, oblongs, and curved lines are all you need to get these elements onto the map. Label each element on the map or number each one, and create a key on a separate piece of paper.

Next, mark human-use areas on the map. If there is a children's play area, for example, fill in the grid squares or area on the map that represents it.

Backyard Flyway Habitat Planting

Homeowners can create flyway habitats for birds by planting a layered landscape along their property lines. Planting in layers from the ground to the tallest trees will invite the widest range of bird species.

The canopy is the level at the tops of the tallest trees.

The understory level of a landscape contains shrubs and small trees.

Ground level plantings are composed of groundcovers and low-growing perennials.

Now, begin marking the major plantings in your existing landscape. If you have a vegetable or herb garden, identify it as such. It's not necessary for this plan to show that you usually have a row of tomatoes here or a patch of basil there. On the other hand, when you come to flower beds, individual trees or shrubs, groundcovers, hedges, and the like, you will want to sketch them onto your map individually and then identify the species individually. For example, if you have a row of eastern white pines along the northern border of your property, you will want to have each one indicated and identified individually.

Simple cloud-shaped outlines can serve as representations for deciduous trees. A starburst-type circle might be your symbol for evergreen trees. A circle with a couple lines drawn through its diameter could represent deciduous shrubs. The exact symbols are your choice. Just make sure you stick with your initial choice to represent similar elements.

The same type of symbol can represent all your deciduous trees, but remember to identify on your key the exact species for each individual tree you sketch. The size of the symbol should correspond roughly to the width of the ground coverage provided by the branches of the tree or shrub when fully leafed out.

As you move across your property mapping the plants, don't overlook the plants you did not intend to grow or never planted, the woodpile you've been meaning to get rid of, and other odd elements like these. They are all part of your existing landscape. You need to know where they are and you need to have them clearly identified.

You may find that symbols often need to overlap. A shade tree covers a part of a play area. A vine is growing up the side of a shed. Let them overlap on your plan. It will show your existing property as it really is.

The final product of your efforts should look much like a cartoonlike aerial view of your property. Now, it's time to add your dreams and hopes to the plan.

Make several photocopies of your map and key. If you've done them in color, you will need to use a color photocopier. You will want to have several copies of both on hand for the next stage, as you will be drawing directly on the map and making changes on the key. Mistakes will happen. You will change your mind as you move along, so those extra copies will come in handy.

Begin re-creating your property; decide which of the existing elements you will keep as they are, which you will remove, which you will enhance, and what you want to add. Draw an X through those elements you want to remove completely. Redraw any elements you want to keep but not where they are now. And then, sketch in any enhancements you might want to make.

You are now ready to project into the future, plan for the addition of completely new elements to your property, and add those crucial new habitat elements. Sketch them right over the existing landscape features or the spots where you have X-ed out existing features.

When adding shrubs to the plan, draw their dimensions in proportion to the size they will be when the plant is fully grown—not the size it will be when you put it into place as a young plant. For trees, draw them to about three-quarters of the mature size. This will give you a more accurate image of what you are working toward and may also help you avoid planting sun-loving plants in a spot that eventually will be under heavy shade. It also can help you avoid future problems between your trees and intrusions such as utility lines and the roofs of buildings.

If you want areas of your property to have a slightly wilder look, appealing to those who landscape for wildlife, leave your old row style of planting in the past. Nature almost never grows wild things in straight lines. Think of your wildlife plantings in circles, or zigzag snakelike patterns, or clusters with scalloped edges. Irregular lines will produce the wilder look you may be seeking. Landscape designers call these irregular planting areas "island beds," and when properly planned out, they are as appealing to people as to wildlife.

Meeting Your Habitat Needs First

As you plan for your new landscape, including the new habitat areas for the birds, remember not to exclude yourself or your family. It is your backyard, and you may come to resent being excluded while still having to do all the work that maintaining a landscape involves.

The need for a play area, swimming pool, deck, patio, picnic table, barbecue pit, parking, and the like, doesn't disappear when you incorporate habitat elements into the landscape. In some cases, habitat elements can gel nicely with human-use areas. Vining, flowering plants can really beautify a fence that was erected to hide trash receptacles, sewer caps, or an older eyesore fence.

It pays to carefully study the lifecycles of plants before siting them. For example, leaf- and litter-dropping deciduous trees branching out over a swimming pool make an equation for constant frustration and continuing labors. An evergreen tree, compact shrub, or small tree that does not extend over the pool would be a better choice.

Matching Habitat to Birds You Want

As explained earlier, the five basic elements of habitat are food, water, shelter from enemies and the elements of weather, a safe and secure place to reproduce and rear young, and space.

Each species of bird meets those five survival needs through its own, unique choices of combinations of plants, water sources, brush piles, stones and boulders, areas of open soil, and so on. If a species is native to a certain area, it still exists there in large enough numbers, and can meet its survival needs, then the populations of that species will flourish and increase.

And, there is an incredible amount of overlap in which multiple species of birds make use of the same landscape elements to meet their individual niche need.

Decide which birds you would like to attract into your backyard. Learn about their habitat needs and preferences and their behaviors. Determine which habitat elements satisfy those needs and preferences. Then, add them to your landscape plan and to your backyard.

In the bird identification chapter, beginning on page 78, we have included information on the habitat needs of dozens of the most common bird species to get you started. A good field guide of birds that includes in-depth discussions about each species would be an eye-opening next step (see Resources on page 168).

Selecting Plants for Bird Food Sources

Most plants from the nonnative exotics offered by the local garden center to the free-growing, wild natives, provide food or shelter for some bird species. It's almost impossible to select a plant that won't have at least some benefit for some bird. However, some plants are better sources of food and nesting habitat for certain birds.

Raspberry and blackberry brambles (*Rubus* spp.) have been documented to be eaten by 145 bird species; elder (*Sambucus* spp.) 120; dogwood (*Cornus* spp.), grape (*Vitis* spp.), and blueberry (*Vaccinium* spp.), more than 90 each; bayberry (*Myrica* spp.) and cherry (*Prunus* spp.), about 85 each; oak (*Quercus* spp.) and pine (*Pinus* spp.), more than 60 each; red cedar (*Thuja plicata*), about 55; and spruce (*Picea* spp.), more than 30.

ALL-SEASON TIP

Birds show individual preferences for various fruit-producing plants, picking those that they like best, cleaning off fruits early in the season, and letting the fruit they find less tasty hang onto other plants. Some fruits, such as persimmons (Diospyros virginiana), *actually become more palatable, softer, and sweeter only after a couple of light autumn frosts. By adding the less-desired plants to your habitat, you'll be stocking the birds' pantry for the late winter, the hardest time of the year, when the berries they passed up previously become life-saving food stores. Some of these plants are bayberry* (Myricca spp.), *beautyberry* (Callicarpa spp.), *hackberry* (Celtis occidentalis), *hawthorn* (Crataegus spp.), *holly* (Ilex spp.), *mountain ash* (Sorbus aucuparia), *sumac* (Rhus spp.), *and viburnum* (Viburnum spp.).

Great Food Plants for Birds

COMMON NAME	BOTANICAL NAME	COMMON NAME	BOTANICAL NAME
EVERGREEN TREES		**DECIDUOUS SHRUBS**	
DOUGLAS FIR	(*Pseudotsuga menziesii*)	BARBERRY	(*Berberis* spp.)
HEMLOCK	(*Tsuga canadensis*)	BAYBERRY, BOG-MYRTLE	(*Myricca* spp.)
HOLLY	(*Ilex* spp.)	BLACKBERRY	(*Rubus* spp.)
JUNIPER	(*Juniperus* spp.)	BLUEBERRY, BILBERRY	(*Vaccinium* spp.)
LARCH	(*Larix* spp.)	BUFFALO BERRY	(*Shepherdia* spp.)
PINE	(*Pinus* spp.)	CURRANT	(*Ribes* spp.)
RED CEDAR	(*Juniperus virginiana*)	DOGWOOD	(*Cornus* spp.)
SPRUCE	(*Picea* spp.)	ELDERBERRY	(*Sambucus* spp.)
		FIRETHORN	(*Pyracantha* spp.)
DECIDUOUS TREES		HAWTHORN	(*Crataegus* spp.)
ALDER	(*Alnus*)	HOLLY	(*Ilex* spp.)
ASH	(*Fraxinus* spp.)	HONEYSUCKLE	(*Lonicera* spp.)
ASPEN	(*Populus* spp.)	INK BERRY	(*Ilex glabra* spp.)
BEECH	(*Fagus*)	JUNEBERRY	(*A. lamarchii* spp.)
BIRCH	(*Betula* spp.)	PRIVET	(*Ligustrum* spp.)
BLACK GUM	(*Nyssa sylvatica*)	SERVICEBERRY	(*Amelanchier ovalis*)
CRAB APPLE	(*Malus sylvestris*)	SUMAC	(*Rhus* spp.)
CHERRY	(*Prunus* spp.)	TRUMPET CREEPER	(*Campsis* spp.)
DOGWOOD	(*Cornus* spp.)	VIBURNUM, DOGBERRY	(*Viburnum* spp.)
HACKBERRY	(*Celtis occidentalis*)	VIRGINIA CREEPER	(*Parthenocissus quinquefolia*)
HICKORY	(*Carya* spp.)		
MAPLE	(*Acer* spp.)	**VINES**	
MULBERRY	(*Morus* spp.)	GRAPE	(*Vitis* spp.)
OAK	(*Quercus* spp.)	GREENBRIER	(*Smilax rotundifolia*)
PECAN	(*Carya illinoinensis*)	HONEYSUCKLE	(*Lonicera* spp.)
PERSIMMON	(*Diospyros virginiana*)		
RED CEDAR	(*Juniperus virginianus* spp.)	**GROUND COVERS**	
		BEARBERRY	(*Arctostaphylos* spp.)
EVERGREEN SHRUBS		CATBRIER	(*Smilax* spp.)
BUCKTHORN	(*Rhamnus* spp.)	CLOUDBERRY	(*Rubus chamaemorus*)
COTONEASTER	(*Cotoneaster* spp.)	DEWBERRY	(*Rubus caesius*)
HOLLY	(*Ilex* spp.)	CROWBERRY	(*Empetrum nigrum*)
HUCKLEBERRY	(*Vaccinium* spp.)	GROUND JUNIPER	(*Juniperus* spp.)
INKBERRY	(*Ilex glabra*)	POKEBERRY	(*Phytolacca americana*)
JUNIPER	(*Juniperus* spp.)	ROSE	(*Rosa* spp.)
RHODODENDRON	(*Rhododendron* spp.)	SARSAPARILLA	(*Smilax officinalis*)
SALAL	(*Gaultheria shallon*)	SERVICEBERRY	(*Amelanchier* spp.)
YEW	(*Taxus* spp.)	STRAWBERRY	(*Fragaria* spp.)
		VIRGINIA CREEPER	(*Parthenocissus quinquefolia*)
		WINTERGREEN	(*Gaultheria procumbens*)

SELECTING PLANTS FOR NESTING AND SHELTER

The northern mocking-bird—welcomed for its ability to imitate an amazing array of sounds from birds and mammals to even music—is most attracted to sites that offer thick shrubs to conceal its nest.

As with food sources, birds can fulfill their nesting and shelter needs with a wide range of plants. Some species restrict themselves to a tight little list of useful plants, but most will take advantage of whatever species of plant presents itself as part of the right habitat. But, because they have evolved to live in "vertical layers," some will prefer low-growing plants, others will inhabit shrubs and understory trees, and others prefer the upper reaches of tall trees.

Plants and the Birds They Attract

OPEN GROUND
Open ground is attractive to a number of ground-dwelling birds. These include the dark-eyed junco, winter wren, hermit thrush, California quail, rock dove, killdeer; and in the United Kingdom and Europe, fieldfare and little owl.

GRASSLANDS
Grasslands interest another set of birds, many of which are colorful and gifted singers:

dickcissel, song sparrow, field sparrow, white-throated sparrow, white-crowned sparrow, savannah sparrow, hermit thrush, eastern blue-bird, western bluebird, very, brown thrasher, red-winged blackbird, eastern meadowlark, common yellowthroat, ring-necked pheasant, northern bobwhite, mallard, and Canada goose and in the United Kingdom and Europe, snipe, meadow pipit, and yellow wagtail.

THICK SHRUBS AND SMALL DECIDUOUS TREES
Many species are attracted to thick shrubs for concealing nests: common redpoll, blue grosbeak, indigo bunting, song sparrow, field sparrow, painted bunting, rufous-sided towhee, bushtit, very, ruby-crowned kinglet, Northern mockingbird, brown thrasher, gray catbird, common grackle, boat-tailed grackle, red-winged blackbird, Brewer's blackbird, white-eyed vireo, black-billed magpie, loggerhead shrike, black-chinned hummingbird, Anna's hummingbird, mourning dove, and common ground dove; and in the United Kingdom and Europe, magpie, dunnock, and black cap.

In small deciduous trees, we're likely to find some favorite backyard birds: rose-breasted grosbeak, brown towhee, house sparrow, black-capped chickadee, Carolina chickadee, Carolina wren, house wren, brown creeper, tufted titmouse, bushtit, American robin, wood thrush, brown thrasher, gray catbird, northern oriole, orchard oriole, common grackle, boat-tailed grackle, red-winged blackbird, Brewer's blackbird, European starling, cedar waxwing, black and white warbler, white-eyed vireo, red-eyed vireo, American redstart, blue jay, tree swallow, violet-green swallow, eastern kingbird, least flycatcher, loggerhead shrike, northern flicker, downy woodpecker, pileated woodpecker, red-headed woodpecker, black-chinned hummingbird, ruby-throated hummingbird, Anna's hummingbird, mourning dove, common ground dove, screech owl, and American kestrel; and in the United Kingdom and Europe, redstart, mistle thrush, and marsh tit.

SMALL CONIFERS
Those species preferring to nest in small conifers are favorites of backyard birdwatchers: northern cardinal, pine siskin, chipping sparrow, black-capped chickadee, Carolina chickadee, Carolina wren, house wren, brown creeper, tufted titmouse, American robin, golden-crowned kinglet, ruby-crowned kinglet, common grackle, European starling, yellow-rumped warbler, black and white warbler, white-eyed vireo, red-eyed vireo, American redstart, blue jay, gray jay, Steller's jay, tree swallow, least flycatcher, loggerhead shrike, mourning dove, and common ground dove, and in the United Kingdom and Europe, sedge warbler and redpoll.

TALL DECIDUOUS TREES
In the taller deciduous trees, we'll find interesting smaller birds as well as a few predatory birds: American goldfinch, house sparrow, black-capped chickadee, white-breasted nuthatch, red-breasted nuthatch, tufted titmouse, blue-gray gnatcatcher, northern oriole, orchard oriole, common grackle, boat-tailed grackle, Brewer's blackbird, European starling, cedar waxwing, yellow-throated warbler, black and white warbler, red-eyed vireo, blue jay, American crow, tree swallow, violet-green swallow, eastern kingbird, least flycatcher, loggerhead shrike, northern flicker, downy woodpecker, pileated woodpecker, red-headed woodpecker, ruby-throated hummingbird, screech owl, American kestrel, and red-trailed hawk; and in the United Kingdom and Europe, great tit and jay.

LARGE CONIFERS
Those species showing a preference for large conifers include some of the birds that also frequent tall deciduous trees: Purple finch, evening grosbeak, red crossbill, black-capped chickadee, white-breasted nuthatch, red-breasted nuthatch, tufted titmouse, golden-crowned kinglet, ruby-crowned kinglet, common grackle, European starling, yellow-rumped warbler, yellow-throated warbler, black and white warbler, red-eyed vireo, blue jay, American crow, tree swallow, least flycatcher, loggerhead shrike, and red-trailed hawk, crossbill, siskin, and treecreeper.

ALL-SEASON TIP

Thick, deciduous shrubs are a favorite nesting choice, and those with thorny branches hold special appeal because they exclude predators. Native shrubs hold still more appeal because they can offer a bonus of edible fruits. But, studies have shown that one popular native landscape shrub, the burning bush (Euonymus Alata), holds a hidden threat to nesting birds. Its stiff branches are sturdy enough for predators to climb, making nests easy prey for house cats. When looking for ideal nesting shrubs, give consideration to those with thin, flexible branches, such as native viburnums (Viburnum spp.). They have a graceful habit; offer flowers in spring and attractive, edible fruits in fall; and their branches cannot support the weight of predators.

Special Habitat Techniques

Many special techniques, some borrowed from traditional gardening and some unique to habitat gardening and landscaping, can be employed by backyard birdwatchers to enhance a property for attraction to and use by birds.

Conservation dead-heading is a variation on the common gardening technique of dead-heading in which a gardener pulls off faded flowers throughout the season to keep a garden bed looking tidy. But, instead of plucking dead heads from flower stems as they begin to fade and go to seed, conservation dead-heading means the habitat-gardener leaves about a quarter of the old flower heads on each plant to go to seed. When the seeds are about ready to drop, we help them fall where we want additional growth of that plant species by crumbling them over the chosen spots.

We still remove about 75 percent of the faded flowers heads as we would with conventional dead-heading to encourage additional flowering over a longer period as the plants force the growing cycle to its extremes. But, with the 25 percent we leave on the stem, we are both planning for the spread of beneficial plants and providing a source of edible seed for the birds.

The brush pile is another landscape feature highly attractive to a wide variety of birds, particularly all those little sparrow and wren species that spend long hours exploring the tangles for their next scrap of food. It can be as simple as a pile of all the clippings collected from your landscape work around your yard that you assemble in some out-of-the-way location at the back of the property. Or, it can be as complex as a planned layering of rows of logs alternating with rows of prunings and small branches. The best brush piles, from wildlife's perspective, are those that allow a honeycomb of open space inside among the elements that make up the brush pile. Those become places where birds can for hide, rest, and escape from predators.

Project: Build Your Own Brush Pile

If you have the space for a brush pile at the back of your property, where it won't visually offend the neighbors, the birds will eagerly welcome the extra protection from the elements and predators. In particular, those small, ground-loving species will spend considerable time hopping through the nooks and crannies inside the pile.

As the name implies, it can be a simple pile of brush made up of all your tree and shrub trimmings, pulled weeds, dead flower plants, or dried tomato and cucumber vines from the vegetable garden. On the other hand, there is a simple construction technique for vastly improving the usefulness of a brush pile for a wide array of wildlife by creating more diverse openings under the pile.

MATERIALS

Seven 5" (13 cm) diameter logs or long tree branches

A pile of garden clippings, twigs, and small branches

Begin with a layer of three parallel logs spaced 1 foot (30 cm) or more apart. Then, top them with a layer of four similar logs, similarly spaced and stacked perpendicular to the first row.

The finished brush pile looks like a dry-land beaver lodge without the mud.

1 Lay down a crisscrossing pattern of 5-inch (13 cm)-diameter logs on the chosen spot.

2 Mound all available sticks, limbs, vines, and such, atop the second layer of logs, allowing them to spill down over the sides of the logs to the ground.

3 Continue adding trimmings from your trees and shrubs to build up the brush pile. As each layer of logs is concealed, put on another log layer, as directed above, until your pile is as high as you can manage.

The pine trees near these feeders create the kind of thick-edged cover that make many small songbirds, such as these goldfinches and northern cardinals, feel safer and more comfortable about visiting the nearby feeders.

Creating a Natural Habitat

The edge is a habitat term for the zone where two different types of habitat (usually vertical layers) come together and blend for a bit, incorporating some plants of each layer. The diversity of birds eager to use an edge area is generally greater than for either of the two habitats on their own. Species that normally occur in both of the converging habitat types can find the elements of their habitat niche within the edge.

Perhaps, at the rear of your property, there is a line of trees and shrubs. Adding a planting area of wildflowers and tall grasses in front of the tree and shrub line will start that area of your property on its way to becoming edge. If you want a more manicured look, you can incorporate this technique into island beds or long planting borders by carefully incorporating groundcovers, shrubs, and a few small trees. Many ornamental plants, such as shrub roses, and flowering trees like redbud, dogwood, and ornamental cherry, also provide stellar habitat for birds.

Snag is the current technical term for what we used to call a hollow tree. Actually it's a dead or dying tree, either hollow in the center or becoming hollowed out, and still standing. It is another magnet for many bird species, particularly the cavity nesters, like owls, and those that eat crevice- and hole-dwelling insects. For habitat gardeners not lucky enough to have a dead tree or two already in their landscape, it is an easy habitat element to create by girdling existing mature or nearly mature trees, 6 to 20 inches (1 to 51 cm) in diameter. Cut a 6" (15 cm)-wide band completely around the tree trunk, removing both the outer and inner barks. That will effectively kill the tree, creating a prime environment for decay to set into the wood and to begin the snag.

The fallen log can become an attractive part of many areas of your residential landscape. It can be either the centerpiece of a landscaping plant cluster or an extra element off to one side of a planting area.

Birdbaths are custom made to meet a bird's bathing needs. They should be shallow enough to allow a bird to stand on the floor, and the bowl should have a rough texture to provide firm footing.

Miniponds and Bigger Ponds

Not only is water a very basic need for birds, but it also can become a true magnet for your property. Water is not nearly as common in the wild environment as we humans imagine. It can often be at a premium, and birds will travel considerable distances to get to it.

Drinking, of course, is the primary use, but many of our common bird species relish a splashing bath when they can get it, and because water attracts many species of animal and insects, the water or water's edge is also a convenient meal-time hunting ground.

Birdbaths, which are among the first considerations for those adding the element of water to their backyard habitat, should be no deeper than 2 inches (5 cm) and not too slippery on the bottom for birds to lose their footing.

If you currently have no water source on or near your property, simply placing a birdbath there, and keeping it clean and filled with fresh water, will attract many more birds and in greater variety than you have now. Plan to clean your birdbath with a stiff brush and to rinse and refill every other day in summer to keep water fresh and prevent diseases spreading among the birds that use it.

ALL-SEASON TIP

To battle ice on pavements and driveways in close proximity to wildlife habitat areas, use sand or ice melting products labeled as non-toxic. Toxic ice-melting products can be deadly to birds, but birds will often ingest the materials because of their salty constituency. Sand, on the other hand, provides good traction on snow and ice, and is also a beneficial substance for birds to eat because it aids food digestion in their food-grinding crops.

The element of moving water, with its accompanying sounds, is a major attraction and can lure birds over a long distance. Here, it's provided by a dripper device suspended over a traditional birdbath.

PROJECT: SIMPLE MOVING WATER

Any basic birdbath can be further enhanced as a supermagnet for birds by adding the sound and sight of moving water. Elaborate and expensive waterfall and fountain arrays are available at all stores and catalogs that sell pond supplies (see Resources, page 168).

MATERIALS

Empty plastic milk or soda bottle

One finishing nail

A length of twine or wire

Wrought-iron shepherd's crook plant hanger (optional)

1 Thoroughly clean and rinse the inside of the bottle.

2 Remove all traces of labels from the outside of the bottle.

3 Remove any plastic collars that may be present around the neck of the bottle that could catch and trap birds' feet.

4 Use a nail to punch a few tiny pinholes into the bottom of the bottle.

5 Attach cord or wire tightly around the neck of the bottle to hang it by.

6 Fill the bottle with water, and seal the cap tightly.

7 Hang the bottle from a tree limb or from a shepherd's crook type plant hanger, suspending it over a birdbath to set the aquatic symphony in motion. You will likely have to refill the bottle daily, but your effort will be rewarded many times over by the increased number of avian visits to your birdbath.

Birds need to feel very secure while bathing since it gets their feathers wet and makes them heavy and temporarily reduces their ability to fly. Raising a birdbath onto a pedestal at least 3 feet (1 m) off the ground gives birds a sense of security over potential predators, such as neighborhood cats. Locating the birdbath a few feet from shrubs or trees with low-hanging branches will offer quick escape cover for the bathing birds from both ground-based and aerial predators such as hawks.

ALL-SEASON TIP

In the heat of summer, birdbaths with water left standing in them for several days can become deadly stews of bacteria and viruses. Every day during the warmest days of the year, make a point of emptying each bath, scrubbing it with a stiff brush, rinsing, and refilling with fresh water. Although nothing more than water is needed for the scrubbing of a birdbath that's being cleaned on a regular schedule, a mix of water and white vinegar will add a little extra umph to the cleaning effort without adding anything harmful to the environment.

Ground-based water sources, ranging from simple pans of water to large and elaborate ponds, are the next step in adding water to your habitat. The larger and more diversified the water source, of course, the greater the variety of birds it will attract.

Many backyard pond owners find dealing with plants in their aquatic environments to be a much easier and more pleasant task if they do their watery planting in individual containers. To keep the soil in the pots, top them with a layer of gravel, held in place by crimping a piece of wire screen, such as chicken wire around the gravel and the pot. (Look for wire mesh with large holes to allow the plant to grow upward).

Selecting Water Plants for Birds

The impact of aquatic plants in attracting birds into our backyard habits is primarily to provide secure spots atop our garden ponds for birds to wade, drink, and bathe. Large-leaved water lilies and water lettuce can provide floating landing pads, as can tangles of floating plants like azolla (*Azolla* spp.), parrot's feather (*Myriophyllum* spp.), and water hyacinth (*Eichhornia crassipes*) and you'll have the added treat of watching frogs and turtles sunning themselves on these floating islands.

4 SPECIAL CONSIDERATIONS

ACHIEVING NATURAL BALANCE IN YOUR HABITAT

Humans like to feel in control of nature, regardless of how true and real that feeling may turn out to be. Some of us may not like to say it, but we resent any part of nature that resists bending to our will. We're willing to expend huge amounts of resources to make the land, and everything on the land, conform to our plan.

That's why we become so agitated when something we plan and execute in the backyard to benefit this species or that species of wildlife goes awry. A deep resentment for an unintended beneficiary of our largesse can smolder in us for years.

We really don't appreciate the only three rules of wildlife habitat work that prove true every time: There's nothing we can do for just one species of wildlife living under wild conditions; at least one, but usually many unintended

species will find a way to benefit, as well; and, every species of wildlife carries some challenges when living in close proximity to humans. There are pluses and a minuses to anything we do to attract wildlife.

One morning, you're dreamily watching a flock of finches at your feeders when you are awakened by a much larger bird that appears out of nowhere, snatches one of the finches, and flies away. A few tiny finch feathers float to the ground.

You intended to provide easy meals for "your" songbirds, but now you've set up a complete web of life, a complete food chain. The finches are finding food where you intended. A hawk is doing what comes natural—finding the food it also needs—but you never intended to provide for the predatory bird, as well.

PREDATORS: PETS AND NATURAL ENEMIES

Predators are a natural result of attracting large numbers of birds into a given area. The hawk we just described eventually turned up in our backyard because our efforts had pulled together an abundance of its prey.

At least it's a natural part of the ecosystem. That hawk is supposed to be there, fulfilling the responsibilities of its niche near the top of the food chain. It serves a purpose, often winnowing out the weak and sick members of the prey population and always helping to keep those prey species from overpopulating.

If the little piles of feathers are too strong an introduction to the natural order of things, the backyard birder can discontinue his or her feeder operation for a short time. The prey species will disperse, and the predator will relocate its hunting grounds to a more fruitful area. After it's all clear, resume filling the feeders.

A few shrubs, placed within an easy dash from the feeder, will help more of the prey birds—those that the birder wants to attract—to escape the talons of a hawk. The raptor will still claim some songbirds, but if the pickings become too difficult, it may relocate its hunting grounds.

A wide range of feeders filled with a carefully chosen selection of seed and food types to attract the maximum variety of bird species is a common method of controlling the environment by backyard birdwatchers.

Free-roaming neighborhood cats are another situation entirely. A growing number of backyard birdwatchers are willing to accept, and even marvel at, the predations of a natural predator, like hawks, but resent wild and native songbirds lost to a feline that isn't a natural part of the ecosystem.

Cats Indoors, the campaign for safer birds and cats, claims that hundreds of millions of wild birds are killed by free-roaming pet cats every year. The group is also concerned about the danger to cats themselves, crossing roadways, encountering wild animal attacks, and being captured by humans who dislike and harm them or collect them for research laboratories.

According to the National Audubon Society, birds constitute about 20 to 30 percent of the prey taken by feral and free-ranging domestic cats. The American Ornithologists' Union, American Association of Wildlife Veterinarians, International Association of Fish and Wildlife Agencies, National Association of State Public Health Veterinarians Inc., and the Cooper Ornithological Society have concluded that free-ranging domestic cats have a serious impact on bird populations and have contributed to the decline of many bird species. Domestic felines may have been involved in the extinction of more bird species worldwide than any other cause with the exception of habitat destruction.

A study in San Diego County, Calif., found that free-roaming cats may have led to the local extinction of several native birds, such as the roadrunner, cactus wren, and California quail. A joint U.S.-Great Britain study showed that a single free-roaming cat can kill as many as 1,000 small animals and birds per year. Cats with bells on their collars often learn to stalk silently even while "belled" and, thus, still kill birds. Even well-fed pet cats give in to their instinct to hunt and kill, which is thought to be a function of a different part of the brain than where hunger originates.

The best solution is for cat owners to keep their pet cats indoors, but there are always those who pity their animals because they believe they need to get outdoors. That means anticat defenses are up to us backyard birdwatchers. We must remove low, dense shrubs from the immediate vicinity of our feeders and water sources, or replace those shrubs with others that carry thorny, or flexible stems, which cats avoid. We can attach the thorny stems of wild roses, blackberries, or strands of barbed wire, to our feeder poles to keep cats from climbing them. And, we must not hang our feeders in locations where cats can get above them.

Discourage Cats

Cats are pretty picky about all elements of their personal space, which gives us many opportunities to persuade them to stay away from our bird feeding areas. Try any or all of the harmless dissuaders described below:

- Felines have a strong dislike of the scent of oranges, so scattering orange peels near a cat's favorite spot to wait in ambush near a feeder may solve the problem. A orange-scented spray repellent can be made by blending orange peels and water in a food processor.

- Another scent that cats dislike is castor oil, which could be used in the same manner.

- Cats dislike erratic noises. You can create this by supplying a tray of dried beans or macaroni in a favorite ambush spot so it will rattle when they walk over it.

- And, of course, cats dislike water. The automatic sprinkler could be set to shower the area of the bird feeders at that time in the day when the neighbor's cat makes his regular rounds of your feeders.

Bird Rescue

Regardless of the measures taken to protect birds from cats, some birds are going to be killed; some are going to be injured; and some baby birds are going to be orphaned by predators.

Increasingly, in more and more jurisdictions, only professionally licensed wildlife rehabilitators can legally help an injured or orphaned songbird. And, even if the average person was allowed to attempt care, chances of success are next to zero. An injured or orphaned bird requires care far in excess of anything most of us are prepared to provide.

Only in rare situations is the parent bird very far out of sight when its newly fledged young leaves the nest. Most orphaned birds we find really are not abandoned at all, and the parent birds will continue to feed them until they master the skills of flight and foraging.

Licensed wildlife rehabilitators have spent long hours and a great deal of effort to learn and perfect what guidebooks appear to make available in a simple read-through.

A local rehabilitator usually can be located through the business or government pages of the telephone directory, at a local or state wildlife agency, or even by calling a local veterinarian. Our best course of action just might be to leave a downed bird where we find it, and let nature handle the situation in due course. Unless there is some direct and immediate threat to the animal in question, such as a predator lurking close by or a pounding rainstorm in progress, we might simply move off a distance and maintain a watch over the bird.

An orphaned young bird almost always has not really been abandoned by its parent. Instead, the adult probably is nearby under cover, hiding and waiting until we leave the immediate area.

Man-Made Hazards

Beyond environmental hazards, such as cats and falls from the nest, our man-made properties bear examination because they may pose a number of dangers to the birds we want to attract. A primary health threat to birds are windows. Not knowing much about glass, the fast-flying birds see a closed window as an opening to fly through rather than a clear, hard surface, particularly when they can see through a house to another window, making them think they can fly in one window and out another. They may also be flying at something they see reflected in the window, such as blue sky, or an image of themselves that they perceive as a rival bird in their territory that they want to attack and chase.

A bird always loses in a collision with a window, being stunned on impact at the very least, and possibly breaking a wing or even being killed instantly.

When it comes to bird-friendly solutions to this problem, having dirty windows can be a good thing because they cut down on reflections and collisions. Screens can also help. Covering windows with shade cloth, which is sold at garden centers and in the gardening sections of home centers, will also cut reflections from windows (and cool the interior of the house). Nature and bird-supply stores and catalogs offer self-adhesive hawk silhouettes for sale, which, when stuck to windows, will chase birds away.

PROJECT: MAKE A WINDOW BIRD–SAFE

f you have a window that birds routinely fly into, it might be made safer for birds by affixing a hawk silhouette to the glass. It's not so much that the shape of the hawk decal will scare off the birds, as it will show them something solid there rather than an implied open space to fly through.

MATERIALS

Stiff white copier paper

Scissors

Laminating plastic, the same size as the paper (available at office and art supply stores)

Double-sided clear tape or a clear suction cup (available at discount and hardware stores)

1 Photocopy the silhouette symbol shown here at actual size onto stiff paper (making it as big as possible on the sheet of paper).

2 Using scissors, cut the silhouette out of the photocop..

3 Seal the silhouette between two sheets of clear, self-adhesive, laminating plastic.

4 Cut the silhouette, in its new protective coating, out of the plastic sheets.

5 Mount the silhouette to the inside of the window glass with double-sided tape or to the outside of the window using a clear suction cup.

In extreme cases, it may be necessary to relocate bird feeders, nest boxes, or water sources when their proximity or angle to a house window is determined to be the problem.

Hawk silhouettes like this one, when adhered to a window, have saved many a bird the danger of a crash with that window.

All bird feeders need regular cleaning to keep them from becoming breeding grounds for disease. Bacteria can build up to dangerous levels and should be cleaned regularly.

Keeping Birds Safe from Bacteria

Occasionally, even our bird feeders pose a threat to the birds, particularly when we cause too many birds to congregate for too long a period in one spot, which can promote the spread of diseases, and when we don't keep our feeders clean.

There four diseases that commonly affect feeder bird species.

- *Salmonellosis* is a general term for any disease in animals and people caused by a group of bacteria known by the Latin name, Salmonella. Birds can die quickly if the *Salmonella* bacteria spread throughout their bodies. Infected birds pass bacteria in their fecal droppings. Other birds get sick when they eat seeds or other food contaminated by the droppings or drink from dirty birdbaths.

- *Trichomonads* are a group of protozoan (one-celled microscopic) parasites that affect a broad variety of animals, including

humans. One *Trichomonads* species afflicts only pigeons and doves, particularly the mourning dove. Birds afflicted with Trichomoniasis typically develop sores in their mouths and throats. Unable to swallow, they drop food or water contaminated with Trichomonads that other birds then consume, thus spreading the disease.

- *Aspergillus fungus* grows on damp feed and in the debris beneath feeders. Birds inhale the fungal spores and the fungus spreads through their lungs and air sacs, causing bronchitis and pneumonia.

- *Avian pox* causes wartlike growths on the featherless surfaces of a bird's face, wings, legs, and feet. The virus that causes pox is spread by direct contact with infected birds, by healthy birds picking up shed viruses on food or feeders, or by insects carrying the virus on their body.

ALL-SEASON TIP

Untold numbers of birds die every year as a result of home and agricultural chemicals both from the birds coming into direct contact with chemicals and from indirect contact through sprayed insects that the birds eat. Birds also through the destruction of their insect-prey population by the pesticides. More environmentally friendly pest-control techniques include natural insect predators like ladybird beetles, toads and lacewings; pest-specific traps; and growing plant species, such as pungent herbs and chrysanthemums, which repel insect pests.

Disease usually can be avoided by following a few simple steps.

- Avoid over crowding by providing ample feeder space. If birds have to jostle each other to reach the food, they are too crowded. This crowding also creates stress, making birds more vulnerable to disease.

- Keep the feeder area clean of waste food and droppings. A broom and shovel can accomplish a lot of good, but a wet-dry vacuum, such as you might use in your garage or workshop, will help even more, pulling spilled seeds from all nooks and crannies of feeders, deck railings, and so forth.

- Provide safe feeders without sharp points or edges. Even small scratches and cuts will allow bacteria and viruses to enter and infect otherwise healthy birds.

- Clean and disinfect feeders regularly. To disinfect, use one part liquid chlorine bleach to nine parts tepid water. Make enough solution to immerse an empty, cleaned feeder completely for two to three minutes. Rinse and allow the feeder to air dry before refilling. Once or twice a month should do, but step up cleaning to a weekly schedule if you notice sick birds at your feeders.

- Discard any bird food that smells musty, is wet, looks moldy, or has fungus growing on it. Disinfect any storage container that held spoiled food and the scoop used to fill feeders by cleaning it with bleach solution described above.

- Keep rodents out of stored food. Mice can carry and spread some bird diseases without being affected themselves. The easiest way to do this is to store bird food in small, galvanized trash cans with handles that clamp the lids on. Don't even think of using plastic cans. Mice can easily gnaw into these and will spoil and scatter seeds.

- Don't wait until you see sick or dead birds to act. With good preventative maintenance, you'll seldom find sick or dead birds at your feeders.

Threats to Habitat

Large-scale threats to birds include habitat destruction, climate change, pollution, persecution, and trade. Each threat, if allowed to continue, is a potential cause of extinction, but providing a backyard habit can make a significant contribution toward preserving many species.

Habitat destruction and deterioration is the biggest single threat to birds all over the world and the main threat facing 52 percent of the threatened bird species, according to Britain's Royal Society for the Protection of Birds.

Rural hedgerows here and abroad are disappearing at an alarming rate, removing vital nest sites and critical food sources. Birds not only conduct day-to-day activities, such as hunting for food and nesting in the shelter of hedgerows, they also seek them out during their migrations and will follow these flyways for miles across open country on their way to and from their wintering sites. Homeowners can provide similar flyway habitats by planting vertical layers of vegetation along property lines, and by encouraging neighbors to do likewise, potentially creating flyways that can extend indefinitely. These hedgerows will not only attract birds but a multitude of small wildlife that migrates, such as the increasingly rare box turtle.

ALL-SEASON TIP

A potential backyard hazard for birds, particularly in the spring when they are looking for suitable nesting spots, is an open chimney on the roof of the house. Larger birds like screech owls and wood ducks can become trapped inside as they explore the potential nesting spot. If your home has a chimney, have it capped with a screened covering and then checked periodically to make sure no openings have developed.

Plowing and draining of meadows and wetlands removes large areas of feeding and nesting areas of bird species such as snipe and redshank. In addition, excessive water abstraction from rivers and underground aquifers is threatening many important wetland bird-habitat sites.

Human activities, primarily energy production and transportation, create increasing quantities of greenhouse gases that change the climate of the planet. Many of the physical mechanisms of global warming, their interactions, and the resulting climate change are not yet fully understood, but the impact on a high percentage of all wildlife species on Earth could be catastrophic. The life cycles of birds, timed to coincide with peak abundance of insects and other suitable food items, as well as cover for nesting, could be disrupted. The natural range of some species will be shifted northward and some species may not be able to react quickly enough to survive. The changing climate can damage breeding and wintering grounds and staging spots along a species' migration route.

Chemical and other waste materials can affect many birds directly or indirectly, and pollution can affect all food chains.

Millions of birds are lost every year to poisoning and unregulated trapping and shooting. Millions more are captured from the wild to be legally and illegally traded around the world as pets. So, everything we can do in our own backyards, our own little pieces of the Earth's overall environment, to help birds and other wildlife becomes all the more important and beneficial with each passing day.

Bird Conservation

Coal miners carried canaries down into their mine tunnels to serve as early warning systems for deadly gases. If the canary died, it was time to get to the surface quickly.

Wild birds today perform a similar purpose in relation to the environment on a larger scale. They've been doing that for centuries, and we are only starting to receive their message. But, improving the environment to save the birds is pretty much the same as saving humans in the long run.

While hedgerows continue to disappear from the agricultural landscape, more and more homeowners—particularly those interested in attracting birds—are incorporating them into appropriate spots on their properties. By encouraging neighbors to plant along property lines, flyways can be extended indefinitely.

BirdLife International is a worldwide partnership of nongovernmental, conservation organizations in more than 100 countries, working to conserve birds, their habitats, and global biodiversity. Every four years, the partnership holds a global meeting to adopt strategies, programs, and policies, and to elect a global council and regional committees. The council appoints a chief executive officer to head a decentralized international secretariat to coordinate the partnership's aims and objectives. To learn more about this organization, see Resources on page 168.

We can begin our efforts by improving the environment in our backyards and attracting and enjoying as many species as we can. On a larger scale, we can involve our neighbors and coworkers, join birding groups, societies, and conservation efforts, and stay informed and active on environmental issues.

5

BIRD IDENTIFICATION

BINOCULARS AND SPOTTING SCOPES

Few birdwatchers stay with the sport for long without adding a pair of binoculars to their arsenal. A well-made pair of binoculars greatly enhances a birdwatcher's ability to locate and identify birds at a distance. The old saying, "You get what you pay for," applies here. Poorly made binoculars could bring more frustration than is worth the money.

Begin your binocular search with an inventory of price ranges at several local stores. Unless money is no object, eliminate the most expensive and the cheapest without further consideration. Now, within the remaining range of prices, settle on your personal price range.

ALL-SEASON TIP

When cleaning the lens of binoculars or a spotting scope, first swab it clean with a soft lens brush. Point the lens downward during the swabbing, and dirt particles are likely to fall off and away from the lens. When you are certain that the grit is gone from the lens, clean it with a good, high-quality, high-tech, microfiber cloth made especially for cleaning lenses. Do not use the cloth that came free with your optical device, but a more expensive cleaning cloth that is available at camera and eyeglass stores.

Return to some of the stores, and investigate the features of each pair of binoculars in your price range.

Each company and each model will offer different features and specialties. The following points are most critical to birdwatching:

- Any quality pair of binoculars will have a set of numbers, such as 7 x 35, printed somewhere on the binocular housing.

- The first number (the one appearing before the "x") is the power or magnification rate of the binoculars. Binoculars with a power of 7x will magnify the image seven times. Most birdwatchers prefer a power of 7x or 8x. because it's the perfect blend of magnification and field of vision for both finding the birds quickly and identifying them in detail.

- The number that appears after the "x" is the size of the objective lens. This is where light enters the binoculars. The larger this number is the better. It signifies a greater ability of the binoculars to gather light, making it easier for birders to spot birds in the early morning and evening hours—their most active feeding times.

- Next, divide the size of the objective lens by the magnification rate, and you'll get the size of the exit pupil. An exit pupil of 2 to 4 is recommended for bright-light situations, while an exit pupil of 4 or 5 is recommended for shady conditions, and a number greater than five is best for dawn and dusk use.

Binoculars and a spotting scope offer a
birdwatcher different features, ranging
from magnification power to ease of use,
which must be compared and factored
into any birder's choice of one or the
other instrument.

Remember that in many species of birds, the brightly colored male takes on a much more subdued coloration outside its mating season. The lemon-yellow male of the American goldfinch is a much duller, almost olive-tinged bird during fall and winter. Seasonal color variations can make the task of bird identification all the more fraught with pitfalls, but a good bird identification guide will include tips on noting seasonal coloration changes.

- Look for tinted lenses. The lenses of high-quality binoculars are coated with a special film to reduce glare inside the lens. Properly coated lenses will appear purple or amber when held at arm's length.

- Field of view is the width of the image seen through the binoculars, usually measured at a viewing distance of 1,000 yards (914.5 m). It's often printed on the binoculars in degrees, which, when multiplied by 52.5 will provide you with the field of view. Many find it easier to locate birds with wide field of view binoculars.

While most of the design factors are the same for binoculars and spotting scopes, scopes offers a range of much higher magnification rates, but they are more expensive and often need tripods or monopods for support.

How to Identify Birds

The process of identifying wild birds in the field can seem daunting to the newcomer, particularly when watching a veteran who is able to walk through a woodland or grassland area and identify every bird he passes with a glance. Just remember that he didn't have that ability when he was a newcomer like you. Only through a great deal of study, and trial and error does a birder ever get to that instantaneous identification state whether it's in his backyard or far afield.

For newcomers, it's best to approach the identification challenge step-by-step by beginning with a process of elimination. First, when you spot a bird that's new to you, eliminate as many of the species you already know from consideration. Then, eliminate bird species that do not commonly occur in the area. To speed up the process, you might mark up your bird identification guide by drawing "x's" through species not common to your area.

You can further eliminate species that are not usually present during the season in which you are birding. After you've removed some species from the field of consideration, then begin working toward identification using five basic: *silhouette, plumage and coloring, behavior, habitat preferences,* and *song.*

With just a little experience, you'll be able to quickly identify the family of a bird species based on the shape of its silhouette (shape and size). To do so, note distinguishing features, such as whether the bird is plump and squat, or slim and sleek, short-tailed or long-tailed, short-legged or long-legged, crested or not. The shape and size of the bird's bill can be an important identifier.

To quickly gauge size, carry a mental comparison chart, such as the one we use in the following identification section. This chart is based on easily recognized birds, such as American goldfinch, house sparrow, European starling, American robin, grackle, and American crow. Phrases like "bigger than a house sparrow, but smaller than a European starling" should become key elements of your identification process.

While it's brightly colored plumage that attracts so many people to bird-watching, it's less colorful *field marks* that make speedy field-identification possible. Field marks include things like contrasting *wing bars* or patches, *breast spots* or bars, *eye lines* or circles, *throat patch, crown stripe, lore* (area between base of beak and eye where the nostril holes are located), and *crest.*

A bird's behavior—how it flies, walks, forages, interacts with others of its kind, interacts with the elements of its environment, and even holds its tail—is the next identification clue.

Habitat type, such as woodland, grassland, or wetland, is another telltale sign. Although there are exceptions to any rule regarding wildlife, birds generally stay in one type of habitat or a mix of predictable habitat types that meet their needs.

Birds have unique songs and calls, and their voice can be all that's needed to identify many of them. However, learning and remembering bird songs for future reference can be challenging. Listening to recorded songs and calls will help. And, lots of time in the field, trying to identify the various songs and calls you hear will take you to the next level of expertise.

ALL-SEASON TIP

Making your first several forays into the world of bird identification in the company of an experienced and capable birder is one of the surest ways to begin the pastime with a favorable experience. Not only will the more experience birder correct your misidentifications, he or she also will help you to learn the intricacies of bird identification. Such birders generally can be found through the local chapter of the National Audubon Society or other local birding club. To maximize sightings, plan your first excursions during the spring mating season or during fall migrations. Consult a bird guide to discover what route your favorite birds travel during migrations.

Bird identification becomes a passion for backyard birdwatchers, and, for many, this leads to a lifelong pursuit of seeing and identifying as many bird species as possible. An essential aid to identifying birds is a pair of binoculars and a good field guide.

COMMON BACKYARD BIRD SPECIES

The bird descriptions that follow are arranged by families. This organization will make it easier to identify them using the size comparison and identity factors listed.

NORTH AMERICAN BIRDS

North America is blessed with a rich and varied population of native birds and seasonal birds that fly north from Mexico and South America to breed or overwinter. The following birds are those with wide distribution, and those that are most popular with backyard birdwatchers, because of their interesting colors, songs, or behaviors.

MALLARD

Anas platyrhynchos, Duck family *(ANATIDAE)*

Only in backyards close to large areas of water can the mallard be considered a backyard bird. But, more developments are encroaching on streams, ponds, rivers, lakes, and wetlands, increasing the number of backyards for mallards to thrive. Nearly every water area already has some ducks because they quickly become trained to return to those spots where the pickings are especially good.

PLUMAGE
Gray, darker along back and tail; white at tail; thin white neck ring; emerald green head and neck; brownish breast; female mottled brown, blue speculum, white tail

BILL
Long, flat, rounded; male greenish-yellow with black tip; female mottled brown and orange

FEET
Palmate, orange

LENGTH
About 24" (61 cm)

RELATIVE SIZE
Larger than American crow

SONG
Various quacks

HABITAT
Waterways of all sorts and adjacent grassy areas

FOOD
Vegetation; at the feeder: if near water, prefers grains and cracked corn on the ground

BREEDING RANGE
United States and Alaska, all but northernmost Canada

WINTER RANGE
United States mostly

AMERICAN KESTREL

Falco aparverius, Falcon family (*FALCONIDAE*)

The American kestrel is the smallest, most common, most widespread, and most colorful of all North American falcons. It preys mostly on insects, but small birds, mammals, and reptiles also are on the menu. House sparrows often become prey when a kestrel sets up house in an urban environment.

PLUMAGE
Red-tan with blue-gray shoulders, wings, and crown; white cheeks, chin, and flanks; black-tipped wings and tail; black earliness and eye lines; black spots throughout

BILL
Short, hooked downward, gray with yellow near face

FEET
Anisodactylous, yellow

LENGTH
About 10" (24.5 cm)

RELATIVE SIZE
American robin

SONG
Sounds like "killy-killy-killy"

HABITAT
Grasslands with mature deciduous trees

FOOD
Insects, small mammals, small birds, and small reptiles; not a feeder bird

BREEDING RANGE
Continental United States and Alaska, southern and central Canada

WINTER RANGE
United States, southern Canada

MOURNING DOVE

Zenaida macroura, Pigeon family (*COLUMBIDAE*)

The mourning dove is one of the most controversial birds in our directory. In some states, it's legally a songbird and protected from hunting; elsewhere it's a game bird, and huge numbers are taken every year. Some would like to see the mourning dove given protection everywhere. However, where it is protected, its numbers quickly grow to pest status while hunting keeps it at a level of abundance. About 80 percent of backyard feeding stations in the United States have mourning doves as part of their daily complement of diners.

PLUMAGE
Buff-gray with a pinkish tint on breast and underside; black spots on lower wings

BILL
Short, sharp, gray

FEET
Anisodactylous, reddish

LENGTH
About 12" (30.5 cm)

RELATIVE SIZE
Grackle

SONG
Sounds like "cooooooo, coooo-ah"

HABITAT
Very widespread, generally in weedy or grassy areas with mature trees

FOOD
Seeds, grains; at the feeder: prefers cracked corn and sunflower seeds

BREEDING RANGE
United States, southern Canada

WINTER RANGE
United States

Ruby-throated Hummingbird

Archilochus colubris, Hummingbird family (*TROCHILIDAE*)

The ruby-throated hummingbird is the only hummingbird occurring regularly east of the Mississippi River in North America. Large numbers of the nectar-dependent species return north before most flowers are in bloom each year. They then spend their early-season days sneaking meals from sap-wells, drilled into tree trunks by yellow-bellied sapsuckers.

PLUMAGE
Metallic green above, lighter below; brighter red chin and throat; female lacks red coloring

BILL
Long, needlelike, black

FEET
Anisodactylous, black

LENGTH
About 3½" (9 cm)

RELATIVE SIZE
Smaller than American goldfinch

SONG
Sounds like the squeak of a mouse

HABITAT
Open, wooded areas

FOOD
Flower nectar, tree sap, and some insects; at the feeder: prefers sugar water

BREEDING RANGE
Eastern United States, southern Canada

WINTER RANGE
Mexico, South America

ANNA'S HUMMINGBIRD

Calypte anna, Hummingbird family *(TROCHILIDAE)*

The Anna's hummingbird was originally confined to just the West Coast of North America. But, growing numbers of hummingbird feeders and backyard plantings of its preferred nectar flowers, fuchsias (*Fuschia* spp.) and eucalyptus (*Eucalyptus* spp.), have expanded its range.

PLUMAGE
Iridescent green above; off-white breast; green-tinted underside; black-tipped wings; red face and throat

BILL
Very long, thin, sharp, slight downward curve, black

FEET
Anisodactylous, black.

LENGTH
About 3½" (9 cm)

RELATIVE SIZE
Smaller than American goldfinch

SONG
A squeaky twittering

HABITAT
Open, wooded, or shrubby areas

FOOD
Flower nectar, small insects; at the feeder: prefers sugar water

BREEDING RANGE
Western United States, southwestern Canada

WINTER RANGE
Southwestern United States, Mexico, and South America

Black-chinned Hummingbird

Archilochus alexandri, Hummingbird family (*TROCHILIDAE*)

The black-chinned hummingbird is the best-known songster of the hummingbird family. Its humanlike whistle of a song can be loud. Black chins, more than any other hummingbird species, often gather in larger numbers in areas of abundant nectar sources.

PLUMAGE
Bright green above, white below with greenish areas; black throat with border of iridescent purple

BILL
Very long, pointed, slight downward curve, black

FEET
Anisodactylous (three toes turned frontward and one toe pointed backward), black

LENGTH
About 3 ½" (9 cm)

RELATIVE SIZE
Smaller than American goldfinch

SONG
High-pitched, shrill chattering

HABITAT
Grassland, shrubby areas

FOOD
Flower nectar, small insects; at the feeder: prefers sugar water

BREEDING RANGE
Western United States, southeastern Canada

WINTER RANGE
Mexico and South America

BROAD-BILLED HUMMINGBIRD

Cynanthus latirostris, Hummingbird family *(TROCHILIDAE)*

The broad-billed hummingbird is quieter and less active than most members of the hummingbird family. Its flight tends to be less hovering and more erratic than most of the others, as well.

PLUMAGE
Green head and body; blue throat; white on underside of tail; bright red at base of bill

BILL
Long, thin, sharp, black

FEET
Anisodactylous, black

LENGTH
About 3¹⁄₂" (9 cm)

RELATIVE SIZE
Smaller than American goldfinch

SONG
A squeaky twittering

HABITAT
Woodlands

FOOD
Flower nectar, small insects; at the feeder: prefers sugar water

BREEDING RANGE
Western United States

WINTER RANGE
Southwestern United States, South America

Blue-throated Hummingbird

Lampornis clemenciae, Hummingbird family *(TROCHILIDAE)*

The blue-throated hummingbird often shows year-to-year loyalty to its favored nesting sites, desiring good protection from rain and sun and close proximity to water.

PLUMAGE
Green below; grayish above; white streaks behind eye; white tips on tail; male has a dull blue throat

BILL
Long, sharp, black

FEET
Anisodactylous, black

LENGTH
About 5½" (14 cm)

RELATIVE SIZE
American goldfinch

SONG
Sounds like "thweep-thweep-thweep"

HABITAT
Woodlands

FOOD
Flower nectar, insects; at the feeder: prefers sugar water

BREEDING RANGE
Southwestern United States

WINTER RANGE
Mexico

YELLOW-BELLIED SAPSUCKER

Sphyrapicus varius, Woodpecker family *(PICIDAE)*

Tree sap constitutes a large portion of the diet of the yellow-bellied sapsucker. The bird drills countless rows of small holes in tree trunks and then drinks the sweet sap. Although they're known to use more than a thousand species of trees as sap sources, the birds show preference for birches, maples, and some pines.

PLUMAGE
Black with white bars and spots across back and wings; white underside with abundant black chevrons; black head with white lines; red crest and chin; female duller and lacks red crest and chin

BILL
Long, pointed, black

FEET
Zygodactylous, light gray

LENGTH
About 8½" (21.5 cm)

RELATIVE SIZE
Between starling and American robin

SONG
Sounds like "tweeeeeeeeeeeeep"

HABITAT
Mature woodlands

FOOD
Sap, insects, fruit; at the feeder: prefers fruit

BREEDING RANGE
Northeastern United States, all but northern-most Canada

WINTER RANGE
Southeastern United States and south

DOWNY WOODPECKER

Picoides pubescens, Woodpecker Family (*PICIDAE*)

A common backyard visitor, downy woodpeckers enjoy visiting sites near trees, and they are among the most widespread woodpecker in North America.

PLUMAGE
Black with white bars near cap and across cheek; broken white bands along wings; off-white breast; bright scarlet patch at back of head

BILL
Long, sharp, gray

FEET
Zyodactyl (two toes pointing forward and two toes pointing backward—common to climbing birds), gray

LENGTH
About 6" (15 cm)

RELATIVE SIZE
House sparrow

SONG
Like the whinny of a horse

HABITAT
Open woodlands

FOOD
Insects; at the feeder: prefers suet, peanut butter, and sunflower seeds

BREEDING AND WINTER RANGE
United States except for southwest, Canada except for northernmost provinces

Red-bellied Woodpecker

Melanerpes carolinus, Woodpecker family (*PICIDAE*)

The population and range of red-bellied woodpeckers has been on the increase for many years because the species adapts well to cavity-nesting sites in human-engineered landscapes and to using backyard feeders, particularly those offering suet. It also spends more time foraging on the ground for its food than most other woodpecker species and makes many caches of gathered food.

PLUMAGE
Black with white bars on back, shoulders, and wings; gray cheeks, breast, and underside; red crown, nape of neck, and patch on belly; female lacks red crown

BILL
Large, short, pointed, black

FEET
Zygodactylous, gray

LENGTH
About 10" (24.5 cm)

RELATIVE SIZE
American robin

SONG
Sounds like "churr, churr, churr"

HABITAT
Woodlands

FOOD
Insects, nuts, fruit; at the feeder: prefers suet, oil-type sunflower seeds, and cracked corn

BREEDING AND WINTER RANGE
United States, west to the Great Plains, except New England

RED-HEADED WOODPECKER

Melanerpes erythrocephalus, Woodpecker family *(PICIDAE)*

The red-headed woodpecker is another of the native cavity-nesting species that has suffered in the face of declining snags for nesting sites and competition for sites now occupied by the European starling. However, against other woodpeckers, it is an aggressive defender of its territory, which includes their nesting site and many caches of nuts, seeds, and berries.

PLUMAGE
Red head and neck; black back, shoulders, wings; white patches on wings; white breast and underside

BILL
Large, short, pointed, white with black at tip

FEET
Zygodactylous, off-white

LENGTH
About 10" (24.5 cm)

RELATIVE SIZE
American robin

SONG
Sounds like "queer, queer, queer," a rather grating sound

HABITAT
Open wooded areas

FOOD
Insects, nuts, fruit; at the feeder: prefers suet, peanut butter, whole peanuts, and oil-type sunflower seeds

BREEDING RANGE
Eastern United States, southern Canada

WINTER RANGE
South America

PILEATED WOODPECKER

Dryocopus pileatus, Woodpecker family *(PICIDAE)*

The pileated woodpecker was traditionally found in deep woods areas. But as North America has grown more open, the species has been able to adapt. Part of the reason for the bird's more widespread status now than at the start of the twentieth century is the large amounts of abandoned farms and near-woodland that many suburban developments have become. It's prime habitat for the species.

PLUMAGE
Black with white face, neck band, and patches on wings; pronounced scarlet crest

BILL
Large, short, conical, pointed, dark gray

FEET
Zygodactylous, black

LENGTH
About 17" (43 cm)

RELATIVE SIZE
Between grackle and American crow

SONG
Sounds like "kick, kick, kick"

HABITAT
Woodlands with plenty of conifers and snags

FOOD
Insects; at the feeder: prefers suet; rare feeder bird

BREEDING AND WINTER RANGE
Eastern United States, west coast of the United States and across to the Rocky Mountains, southern and central Canada

NORTHERN FLICKER

Colaptes auratis, Woodpecker family *(PICIDAE)*

The northern flicker occurs in three major races across North America: yellow-shafted in the east; red-shafted in the west; and gilded species in the southwest. Until interbreeding studies proved them to be the same species, each was considered a separate species. Regardless of the race, the northern flicker will opt for insects over other sources of food. That characteristic has made the woodpecker more highly adaptable to human settings than most other flicker species.

PLUMAGE
Grayish brown back, wings, and tail with many black dashes; white breast and underside with many black spots and chevrons; large black band at base of throat; bluish gray cap and back of neck; bright scarlet patch under eye

BILL
Long, pointed, gray

FEET
Zygodactylous, gray

LENGTH
About 12" (30.5 cm)

RELATIVE SIZE
Grackle

SONG
Sounds like "wick-a, wick-a, wick-a"

HABITAT
Open woodlands and residential areas with mature deciduous trees

FOOD
Ants, insects, berries; at the feeder: prefers suet; a rare feeder bird

BREEDING RANGE
All of North America, except northernmost Canada and northernmost Alaska

WINTER RANGE
United States, west coast of Canada

PURPLE MARTIN

Progne subis, Swallow family *(HIRUNDINIDAE)*

The purple martin was the first North American bird that humans made nest boxes for. Native Americans dried and hollowed gourds, cut entrance holes in them, and hung them around their crops to attract the insect-eating birds. Natural gourds and imitations of the grounds are gaining popularity today as nest boxes for the species as a valuable tool for insect control. Although the rules about purple martins may be changing as more is learned about the species, in general, the most successful martin house are in close proximity to a pond or lake and surrounded by grassy, weedy areas.

PLUMAGE
Dark blue to purple

BILL
Short, rounded, blue-black

FEET
Anisodactylous, blue-black

LENGTH
About 8" (20 cm)

RELATIVE SIZE
Between house sparrow and European starling

SONG
Sounds like "tea-tea-tea"

HABITAT
Grasslands near stands of trees and water

FOOD
Insects; not a feeder bird

BREEDING RANGE
United States, east of the Rockies and along the West Coast

WINTER RANGE
South America

TREE SWALLOW

Tachycineta bicolor, Swallow family (*HIRUNDINIDAE*)

Tree swallows often play with feathers in the air, diving onto the feather, clasping it in their bills, releasing it, and repeating the game again. Fledglings continue to beg parents for food for awhile after leaving the nest.

PLUMAGE
Dark, metallic, green-blue above; white below

BILL
Short, rounded, black

FEET
Anisodactylous, black

LENGTH
About 6" (15 cm)

RELATIVE SIZE
House sparrow

SONG
Rolling twitter

HABITAT
Grasslands with scattered snags and water

FOOD
Insects, berries; not a feeder bird

BREEDING RANGE
Northern United States and Alaska, southern and central Canada

WINTER RANGE
Usually southern United States but sometimes farther north as well

BLUE JAY

Cyanocitta cristata, Crow family (*CORVIDAE*)

The blue jay is the announcer of the forest. The bird's call announces the movements of everything from squirrels to deer to humans. They even announce their own travels, which are rather clocklike. A birder usually knows of their approach before they arrive at the feeder, usually the same time every day. They are bullies, but they move around often.

PLUMAGE
Bright blue crest, neck, back, wings, and tail; white and gray bars on wings and tail; white face and cheeks; neck ring of black; off-white underside

BILL
Long, conical, black

FEET
Anisodactylous, black

LENGTH
About 12" (30.5 cm)

RELATIVE SIZE
Grackle

SONG
Sounds like "jay, jay, jay" and "ca-weedle, ca-weedle, ca-weedle"

HABITAT
Deciduous woodlands and residential areas with mature deciduous trees

FOOD
Nuts, large seeds, insects, spiders; at the feeder: prefers whole peanuts, whole nuts, oil-type sunflower seeds. During the breeding season, they can prey on disabled birds and sometimes raid other birds' nests, and feed nestlings to their own young.

BREEDING AND WINTER RANGE
All United States and southern Canada, east of the Rockies

GRAY JAY

Perisoreus Canadensis, Crow family (*CORVIDAE*)

The gray jay is a blatant, persistent thief. Any food item put out in its territory is fair game from a picnic lunch to an open hiker's backpack to a piece of game just shot by a hunter. The bird is completely unafraid of most other living things, including humans, and will snatch the food right out of an outdoor diner's hand or a hot frying pan. Hard items like seeds and nuts often are stored even if they're acquired during the winter months when the bird should be drawing on its caches.

PLUMAGE
Gray above; darker at cap, eye line, and nape of neck; grayish white cheeks, breast, and underside

BILL
Long, conical, black

FEED:
Anisodactylous, dark gray

LENGTH
About 12" (30.5 cm)

RELATIVE SIZE
Grackle

SONG
Sounds like "wee-ah, chuck-chuck"

HABITAT
Coniferous woodlands

FOOD
Varied; at the feeder: prefers seeds, cracked corn, and suet

BREEDING AND WINTER RANGE
Northwestern continental United States and Rocky Mountain region, Alaska, and southern and central Canada

STELLER'S JAY

Cyanocitta stelleri, Crow family (CORVIDAE)

The Steller's jay is a bird of routine. It travels the same route every day, from one feeding site to the next, on nearly the same schedule, collecting food and caching most of it close to where it was found. Pine nuts and acorns are favorite foods and raiding the caches of acorn woodpeckers is a favorite activity. Like it's eastern cousin, the blue jay, the Steller's jay announces its travels and the travels of all other creatures it encounters almost constantly.

PLUMAGE
Crested black head; gray breast and shoulders; slate gray wing tips and tail; bright blue elsewhere

BILL
Long, conical, silvery

FEET
Anisodactylous, silverish

LENGTH
About 11" (28 cm)

RELATIVE SIZE
Grackle

SONG
Sounds like "jay, jay, jay" and "ca-weedle, ca-weedle, ca-weedle"

HABITAT
Mixed woodlands that include some conifers

FOOD
Fruit, seeds, nuts, insects; at the feeder: prefers nuts, oil-type sunflower seeds, and cracked corn

BREEDING AND WINTER RANGE
Western continental United States, western Canada, southeastern Alaska

GREEN JAY

Cyanocorax yncas, Crow family (*CORVIDAE*)

The green jay, the only green-colored jay, is one of thirty or so species that makes the lower Rio Grande Valley of Texas a destination for birdwatchers from around the world. It lives in small family flocks of four to nine birds that are fiercely territorial and homebodies to a fault. Only one pair of the birds in each family flock will carry out breeding activities.

PLUMAGE
Bright green body, darker wings; face, neck and breast black; brilliant blue crown and cheeks

BILL
Long, conical, black

FEET
Anisodactylous, brown

LENGTH
About 12" (30.5 cm)

RELATIVE SIZE
Grackle

SONG
Sounds like "jay-jay-jay-jay"

HABITAT
Dense thickets and adjoining agricultural and residential areas

FOOD
Fruit, seeds, insects; at the feeder: prefers corn

BREEDING AND WINTER RANGE
Texas and southward into South America

BLACK-CAPPED CHICKADEE

Parus atricapillus, Titmouse family *(PARIDAE)*

The black-capped chickadee is one of the most regular feeder visitors. At nearly the same time every day, the same flock will appear at the same feeders, making their daily rounds of all available food sources in the neighborhood.

PLUMAGE
Black cap and chin; white cheek stripe; gray shoulders and back; gray wings tipped with white; buff underside

BILL
Short, sharp, black

FEET
Anisodactylous, dark gray

LENGTH
About 5½" (14 cm)

RELATIVE SIZE
Between American goldfinch and house sparrow

SONG
"Fee-bee-bee"

HABITAT
Woodlands, residential areas

FOOD
Insects, spiders, seeds, fruit in winter; at the feeder: prefers oil-type sunflower seeds, suet, and peanut butter

BREEDING RANGE
Northern continental United States and Alaska, central and southern Canada

WINTER RANGE
Shifts a bit to the south of the breeding range

TUFTED TITMOUSE

Parus bicolor, Titmouse family *(PARIDAE)*

The tufted titmouse likes to be part of mixed flocks of small birds, often including chickadees, that visit backyard feeders every day during winter. With the tendency for constant vigilance of the titmouse, its alarm calls become the default alarm system for the entire mixed flock.

PLUMAGE
Gray cap, back, and wings; white around large black eye; red-brown along sides and rump

BILL
Short, conical, black

FEET
Anisodactylous, light gray

LENGTH
About 6" (15 cm)

RELATIVE SIZE
House sparrow

SONG
Sounds like "here-a, here-a, here-a"; or simple "here, here, here"

HABITAT
Woodlands, residential areas

FOOD
Insects, spiders, seeds, fruits; at the feeder: prefers peanut butter, peanut hearts, suet, and oil-type sunflower seeds

BREEDING AND WINTER RANGE
Eastern United States

RED-BREASTED NUTHATCH

Sitta canandensis, Nuthatch family (SITTIDAE)

To many backyard birdwatchers in North America, it appears that the population of red-breasted nuthatches varies widely from year to year. What they're actually observing is the influx of birds from the north into their local populations when the natural seed crop of the northern Canadian forest suffers a failure or is insufficient.

PLUMAGE
White face with black eye lines and cap; gray back, wings, and tail with some black at edge of wing and tail feathers; reddish underside

BILL
Long, sharp, black

FEET
Anisodactylous, dark gray

LENGTH
About 4½" (11.5 cm)

RELATIVE SIZE
American goldfinch

SONG
Sounds like the words "yank, yank"

HABITAT
Coniferous woodlands; agricultural and residential areas in winter

FOOD
Insects, seeds, fruit; at the feeder: prefers sunflower seeds, suet, and peanut butter

BREEDING RANGE
Western and northern United States; south and central Canada

WINTER RANGE
Similar to breeding range, but farther south into the United States

WHITE-BREASTED NUTHATCH

Sitta carolinensis, Nuthatch family (*SITTIDAE*)

While most birds prone to climbing trees head up the trunk, the white-breasted nuthatch typically moves downward and headfirst. This gives the species a special feeding niche, as it looks at cracks and crevices in the bark from a different perspective. Its unique feeding style also makes it an amusing feeder visitor.

PLUMAGE
White face and breast; black cap and back of neck; blue-gray back, wings, and tail

BILL
Long, sharp, blue-gray

FEET
Anisodactylous, dark gray

LENGTH
About 5" (12.5 cm)

RELATIVE SIZE
American goldfinch

SONG
Sounds like "why-why-why" and "ank-ank-ank"

HABITAT
Woodlands; residential areas in winter

FOOD
Insects, seeds, nuts, fruits; at the feeder: prefers sunflower seeds, suet, and peanut butter

BREEDING AND WINTER RANGE
United States, Canada

Brown Creeper

Certhis Americana, Creeper family (CERTHIIDAE)

The brown creeper hunts for insects in the crevices of tree bark, moving up the trunk in a constant spiral and then launching off to glide down to the bottom of an adjacent tree.

PLUMAGE
Tan, brown, and black above with streaking of white on cap; gray eyebrows, chin, breast, and underside

BILL
Long, pointed, brown with white edges

FEET
Anisodactylous, gray

LENGTH
About 5½" (14 cm)

RELATIVE SIZE
Between American goldfinch and house sparrow

SONG
Sounds like "tsee, tsee, tsee"; also a low warble

HABITAT
Woodlands; residential areas in winter

FOOD
Insects and spiders; not much of a feeder bird, but sometimes comes to peanut butter

BREEDING RANGE
Northern continental United States and Alaska; southern and central Canada

WINTER RANGE
United States, southern Canada

HOUSE WREN

Troglodytes aedon, Wren family (*TROGLODYTIDAE*)

The house wren will make use of nearly any nest box of any size that it can find. Then, it fills all other empty nest boxes in the vicinity with false nests that it never uses as a way of confusing predators.

PLUMAGE
Gray-brown above; darker speckling on head; dark stripes on wings and tail; buff breast and underside

BILL
Long, sharp, dark gray

FEET
Anisodactylous, light brown

LENGTH
About 5" (12.5 cm)

RELATIVE SIZE
American goldfinch

SONG
Like the rising and falling of a babbling brook

HABITAT
Woodland edges, agricultural areas, residential areas

FOOD
Insects, spiders; at the feeder: prefers suet and peanut butter

BREEDING RANGE
United States, southern Canada

WINTER RANGE
Southern United States

CAROLINA WREN

Thryothorus ludovicianus, Wren family (*TROGLODYTIDAE*)

The Carolina wren, an intense homebody of a bird, builds its nest in unusual locations, including mailboxes, pockets in jeans hanging on washlines, and outdoor decorations, to name a few.

PLUMAGE
Brown above; buff below; white line above each eye

BILL
Long, sharp, gray

FEET
Anisodactylous, silver-gray

LENGTH
About 5½" (14 cm)

RELATIVE SIZE
American goldfinch

SONG
Sounds like "wee-kettle, wee-kettle, wee-kettle"

HABITAT
Brushy woodlands and fields

FOOD
Insects, spiders, seeds in winter; at the feeder: prefers suet, peanut butter, and oil-type sunflower seeds

BREEDING AND WINTER RANGE
Eastern North America

EASTERN BLUEBIRD

Sialia sialis, Thrush family *(TURDIDAE)*

Backyard birdwatchers have recently saved the Eastern bluebird from near extinction. The population of the species spiraled downward through the middle of the twentieth century as changing agricultural practices removed the fencepost and snags the species needs as nesting sites and exposed the species to deadly pesticides and nonnative competitors for remaining nesting spaces. Birdwatchers turned that trend around by placing hundreds of thousands, maybe millions, of bluebird boxes across the landscape. The species made a major recovery.

PLUMAGE
Bright blue above; red-brown breast fading to off-white underside; female is duller

BILL
Short, pointed, brownish

FEET
Anisodactylous, black

LENGTH
About 7" (18 cm)

RELATIVE SIZE
Between house sparrow and European starling

SONG
Series of soft whistles broken by chatter

HABITAT
Fields with scattered trees

FOOD
Insects, spiders, some seeds, fruits; not much of a feeder bird

BREEDING RANGE
Eastern United States, southeastern Canada

WINTER RANGE
Southeastern United States

WESTERN BLUEBIRD

Sialia mexicana, Thrush family *(TURDIDAE)*

The western bluebird never suffered the population decline of its eastern cousin since it made its home in woodlands and deserts rather than agricultural areas. However, in many parts of its range today, nesting holes are in short supply, and the species will make ready use of bluebird boxes.

PLUMAGE
Dark blue above and on throat; red-brown breast and back; white underside; female
is duller

BILL
Long, pointed, black

FEET
Anisodactylous, black

LENGTH
About 7" (18 cm)

RELATIVE SIZE
Between house sparrow and European starling

SONG
Series of soft whistles broken by chatter

HABITAT
Bushy areas, thickets, woodland edges

FOOD
Insects, spiders, some fruits; not much of
a feeder bird

BREEDING RANGE
Western United States, southwestern Canada

WINTER RANGE
Southwestern United States

AMERICAN ROBIN

Turdus migratorius, Thrush family (*TURDIDAE*)

The American robin has a reputation as a reliable harbinger of spring. However, in most parts of the United States, some robins are present year-round. So, the "first robin of spring" is often just the robin that's been living in a nearby wooded area all winter and has now shown up in the backyard.

PLUMAGE
Black head with white at eyes; dark gray neck, back, wings, and tail; orange-red breast; off-white underside

BILL
Long, rounded, yellow-orange

FEET
Anisodactylous, gray-brown

LENGTH
About 10" (24.5 cm)

RELATIVE SIZE
American robin

SONG
Sounds like "cheer-e-ly, cheer-ip, cheer-e-ly"; also "tut, tut, tut"

HABITAT
Grassy, residential, agricultural, and woodland areas

FOOD
Earthworms, insects, spiders; fruit, berries in winter; at the feeder: prefers fruit

BREEDING RANGE
All but southernmost United States and northernmost Canada

WINTER RANGE
Southern United States with many exceptions farther north

NORTHERN MOCKINGBIRD

Mimus polyglottos, Mimic thrush family (*MIMIDAE*)

The northern mockingbird is extremely protective against nearly all other birds—and many other creatures—within its territory. It will crash right into any perceived usurper with wings flashing at the slightest provocation. Understandably, the bird is aggressive in defending its nesting site, but it also applies the same defensive posturing to feeders that it rarely uses and other spots where it usually shows little or no interest. So aggressive is the species that after the nest of young has emptied, only one of the parent birds will remain in the nesting area.

PLUMAGE
Gray above face, breast, and underside; darker brown-gray wings and tail feathers with white edges; white wing bands

BILL
Long, sharp, slight downward curve, black

FEET
Anisodactylous, yellowish-brown

LENGTH
About 10½" (26.5 cm)

RELATIVE SIZE
Between American robin and grackle

SONG
Mimickry of the songs of other bird species

HABITAT
Grasslands, residential areas, particularly those with brush, thickets, and hedgerows

FOOD
Fruit, seeds, insects, spiders; at the feeder: prefers oil-type sunflower seeds, peanut hearts, and fruit; a rare feeder bird

BREEDING RANGE
United States, southern Canada

WINTER RANGE
United States

CEDAR WAXWING

Bombycilla cedrorum, Waxwing family *(BOMBYCILLIDAE)*

The cedar waxwing is among the last North American species to nest, waiting for wild fruit and berries to ripen since they make up the nestlings' diet. Fruit and berries are eaten by the parents and regurgitated to the nestlings.

PLUMAGE
Greenish-brown with black mask; red waxy-looking tips on wing feather; yellow tips on tail feathers

BILL
Short, rounded, black, slight downward curve

FEET
Anisodactylous, black

LENGTH
About 7" (18 cm)

RELATIVE SIZE
Between house sparrow and European starling

SONG
Sounds like "zeee, zeee, zeee, zeee."

HABITAT
Orchards, woodlands, residential areas; especially those with fruit and berry sources

FOOD
Berries, seeds, insects; not a feeder bird

BREEDING RANGE
Northern United States, southern Canada

WINTER RANGE
All but northernmost United States

EUROPEAN STARLING

Sturnus vulgaris, Starling family (*TURNIDAE*)

The European starling has played a part in the decline of several cavity-nesting bird species, such as the Eastern bluebird. The nonnative North American bird is an aggressive and successful competitor against native species. The European starling was introduced to the United States in 1890–91 by Shakespeare fans who wanted to import all the bird species mentioned in his plays.

PLUMAGE
Black with brownish tint and white flecks throughout

BILL
Long, pointed, bright yellow

FEET
Anisodactylous, orange

LENGTH
About 8" (20 cm)

RELATIVE SIZE
European starling

SONG
Sounds like a series of clicks and squeaks

HABITAT
Residential and agricultural areas

FOOD
Seeds, fruits, insects, spiders; at the feeder: prefers cracked corn and sunflower seeds

BREEDING AND WINTER RANGE
United States, south and central Canada

NORTHERN CARDINAL

Cardinalis cardinalis, Cardinal family *(EMBERIZIDAE)*

The northern cardinal is the most prized of backyard feeders in those regions of the United States where it lives. The brilliant red donned by male northern cardinals, particularly during mating season, is a rare commodity in nature. Instinctively, northern cardinals realize how their vibrant color makes them visible to predators—particularly hawks. So, they tend to stay within close proximity to dense trees or shrubs.

PLUMAGE
Bright red with black face; female buff brown with red at crest, eyes, tips of wings, and tail

BILL
Short, conical, red

FEET
Anisodactylous, gray

LENGTH
About 7½" (19 cm)

RELATIVE SIZE
Between house sparrow and European starling

SONG
Sounds like "wheat-wheat-wheat" and "chip"

HABITAT
Brushy areas, thickets, woodland edges

FOOD
Seeds, some insects, and spiders; at the feeder: prefers oil-type sunflower seed

BREEDING AND WINTER RANGE
Eastern and southwestern United States

ROSE-BREASTED GROSBEAK

Pheucticus ludovicianus, Cardinal family *(EMBERIZIDAE)*

Although the rose-breasted grosbeak's heavy, powerful bill enables the bird to easily crack open seeds, it prefers softer fruit, fruit blossoms, and insects. For a bird not built like an insect eater, it includes a high proportion of insects in its diet.

PLUMAGE
Black head; wings and tail with white patches; rose breast; white sides and belly; female streaked brown and white with white eyebrows

BILL
Large, conical, silver

FEET
Anisodactylous, reddish-gray

LENGTH
About 8" (20 cm)

RELATIVE SIZE
Starling

SONG
Sounds like a series of brief and abrupt whistles

HABITAT
Fields with shrubs and old orchards

FOOD
Fruits, seeds, insects, spiders; at the feeder: prefers oil-type sunflower seeds

BREEDING RANGE
Northern United States and southward along the Appalachian Mountains, southern and central Canada

WINTER RANGE
South of the United States

BLACK-HEADED GROSBEAK

Pheucticus melanocephalus, Cardinal family (*EMBERIZIDAE*)

Male black-headed grosbeaks share incubation time on the nest with their much duller-colored mates even though their brighter markings make them an easy target for predators. It's not as risky as it sounds because most of the male's bright colors are on its breast and underside, which are hidden while sitting on a nest.

PLUMAGE
Black head, back, and wings; orange underside; white wing bars and patches; female buff head, back and wings; dark gray underside

BILL
Large, conical, black

FEET
Anisodactylous, black

LENGTH
About 8" (20 cm)

RELATIVE SIZE
Starling

SONG
Sounds like a series of brief and abrupt whistles

HABITAT
Woodlands

FOOD
Seeds, fruits, insects, spiders; at the feeder: prefers oil-type sunflower seeds

BREEDING RANGE
Western United States, southwestern Canada

WINTER RANGE
Mexico

PINE GROSBEAK

Pinicola enucleator, Cardinal family *(EMBERIZIDAE)*

The pine grosbeak is the largest of the northern finches. It is a rewarding bird to attract to the backyard because it's also a species generally unafraid of humans.

PLUMAGE
Dull reddish body; dark streaks on back and wings; white wing bars; female gray body with dull reddish on head and rump

BILL
Large, conical, gray

FEET
Anisodactylous, dark gray

LENGTH
About 8½" (21.5 cm)

RELATIVE SIZE
Between starling and American robin

SONG
Series of twittering whistles

HABITAT
Woodland

FOOD
Seeds, fruits, buds; occasional feeder bird

BREEDING RANGE
Northern New England and mountain regions of western United States, all but northernmost Canada

WINTER RANGE
Mountain regions of western United States, southern and central Canada

INDIGO BUNTING

Passerina cyanea, Cardinal family (*EMBERIZIDAE*)

Without barbs on the indigo bunting's feathers, the male would appear dark brown. However, the barbs scatter all wavelengths of light except blue, to give our eyes the appearance of nature's deepest blue bird.

PLUMAGE
Bright blue with black on wings, tail, and rump; female gray-brown above, streaked gray and off-white underside

BILL
Large, conical, black

FEET
Anisodactylous, dark gray

LENGTH
About 5½" (14 cm)

RELATIVE SIZE
Between American goldfinch and house sparrow

SONG
Sounds like "tea, to-you, to-you; chew, tea, tea, to-you, to-you"

HABITAT
Brushy areas, old agricultural areas, woodland edges

FOOD
Insects, spiders, seeds, fruit in winter; not much of a feeder bird

BREEDING RANGE
Eastern United States, southern Canada

WINTER RANGE
Central America

RUFOUS-SIDED TOWHEE

Pipilo erythrophthalmus, Sparrow family *(EMBERIZIDAE)*

When foraging through the leaf litter on the forest floor, the rufous-sided towhee creates more sight and sound than any other bird its size. Kicking with both feet, the small bird sends showers of leaf litter into the air. Often heard before it is seen, as it forages, the towhee's noise level often creates the expectation of a much bigger bird or mammal.

PLUMAGE
Black head, back, wings, and tail; red-brown sides; white belly; white wing and tail patches; female light gray-brown above, red-brown sides and white belly

BILL
Short, conical, black

FEET
Anisodactylous, dark gray

LENGTH
About 8½" (21.5 cm)

RELATIVE SIZE
Between starling and American robin

SONG
Sounds like "drink-your-tea, drink-your-tea," ending with a trill

HABITAT
Brushy areas, thickets, woodland edges

FOOD
Seeds, fruits, insects, spiders; at the feeder: prefers sunflower seeds, cracked corn, and peanut kernels

BREEDING RANGE
United States, except Great Plains; southern Canada

WINTER RANGE
United States, southwestern Canada

SONG SPARROW

Melospiza melodia, Sparrow family (*EMBERIZIDAE*)

The song sparrow is one of the most common and widespread bird species in North America, varying widely in coloring and song from one region to the next. It also has one of the largest song repertoires with males capable of producing a thousand variations of twenty song patterns.

PLUMAGE
Streaked gray, brown, and black with noticeably more brown on wings and tail

BILL
Short, sharp, gray

FEET
Anisodactylous, gray-brown

LENGTH
About 6" (15 cm)

RELATIVE SIZE
House sparrow

SONG
Sounds like "maid, maid, maid, put-your-tea, kettle, kettle, kettle"

HABITAT
Thickets, meadows, residential areas

FOOD
Seeds, insects, spiders; at the feeder: prefers oil-type sunflower seeds and proso millets

BREEDING RANGE
Northern and western continental United States, southern and central Canada, southern Alaska

WINTER RANGE
United States, and west coast of Canada

FIELD SPARROW

Spizella pusilla, Sparrow family (*EMBERIZIDAE*)

A denizen of weedy, overgrown areas, the field sparrow has seen a population boom and an expansion in its range as agricultural areas are no longer in production or have been converted into suburban developments.

PLUMAGE
Gray face; red-brown cap; white eye ring; streaked tan, dark brown, and slate along back and wings; buff underside

BILL
Short, conical, pink

FEET
Anisodactylous, bright pink

LENGTH
About 5½" (14 cm)

RELATIVE SIZE
Between American goldfinch and house sparrow

SONG
Sounds like a rapid whistle, ending in a trill

HABITAT
Overgrown agricultural areas

FOOD
Seeds, fruits, insects, spiders; at the feeder: prefers oil-type sunflower and niger seeds

BREEDING RANGE
Eastern United States

WINTER RANGE
South of the breeding range

WHITE-THROATED SPARROW

Zonotrichia albicollis, Sparrow family *(EMBERIZIDAE)*

When a flock of white-throated sparrows discovers a backyard with a steady source of food and thick, shrubby cover nearby, it will set up residence for the winter and remain as long as the food lasts.

PLUMAGE
Streaked tan and black; head striped black and white; gray underside; white throat

BILL
Short, sharp, dark gray

FEET
Anisodactylous, pinkish-brown

LENGTH
About 6½" (16.5 cm)

RELATIVE SIZE
Between house sparrow and European starling

SONG
Sounds like "tooo ti-ti-ti, teee ti-ti-ti, ti-ti-ti, ti-ti-ti"

HABITAT
Coniferous woodlands, brushy areas, residential areas in winter

FOOD
Seeds, insects, spiders; at the feeder: prefers oil-type sunflower seeds

BREEDING RANGE
Northeastern United States, southern and central Canada

WINTER RANGE
Eastern United States

WHITE-CROWNED SPARROW

Zonotrichia leucophrys, Sparrow family (*EMBERIZIDAE*)

The white-crowned sparrow can be conditioned to take seed from human hands with relatively little effort and in a relatively short amount of time. All that's required is to sit still for 10 to 15 minutes with hands cupped upward and filled with seed that white-crowned sparrows enjoy.

PLUMAGE
Streaked tan and black across back and wings; head striped black and white; gray underside; white crown

BILL
Short, sharp, pink

FEET
Anisodactylous, reddish-brown

LENGTH
About 7" (18 cm)

RELATIVE SIZE
Between house sparrow and European starling

SONG
Sounds like a series of whistles followed by "bzzzzzt"

HABITAT
Grasslands, woodlands, residential areas

FOOD
Insects, spiders, seeds in winter; at the feeder: prefers proso millets and sunflower seeds

BREEDING RANGE
East Coast and Rocky Mountain regions of continental United States and Alaska, Canada

WINTER RANGE
United States, southern Canada

DARK-EYED JUNCO

Junco hyemalis, Sparrow family (*EMBERIZIDAE*)

At one time, different regional populations of the dark-eyed junco—with wide-ranging variations in their coloring—were considered separate species. But more recent studies of their interbreeding—wherever their ranges meet—have proven them all to be one species.

PLUMAGE
Gray to gray-brown above; white belly and underside of tail

BILL
Short, rounded, pink

FEET
Anisodactylous, gray

LENGTH
About 5½" (14 cm)

RELATIVE SIZE
Between American goldfinch and house sparrow

SONG
Burry trill

HABITAT
Woodland, residential, and agricultural areas

FOOD
Insects, spiders, seeds in winter; at the feeder: prefers niger seeds, cracked corn, proso millet

BREEDING RANGE
Northern continental United States, all but northernmost Canada and Alaska

WINTER RANGE
United States, southern Canada

COMMON GRACKLE

Quiscalus quiscula, Blackbird family *(ICTERIDAE)*

The common grackle is a big, aggressive bird that instantly takes over any site the flock enters. Smaller birds are bullied and even killed as well as small mammals and reptiles. However, it has one of the most generalist appetites of any North American backyard bird and prefers to feed on the ground. That's good news for backyard birdwatchers, as the grackle will settle for the cheapest seeds simply tossed on the ground while leaving feeders filled with more expensive seed alone.

PLUMAGE
Black with iridescent green-blue to purple tint; wedge-shaped tail

BILL
Long, pointed, black

FEET
Anisodactylous, black

LENGTH
About 12" (30.5 cm)

RELATIVE SIZE
Grackle

SONG
Sounds like "ti-chack"

HABITAT
Open grassy and shrubby areas

FOOD
Insects, spiders, seeds; at the feeder: has wide-ranging diet

BREEDING RANGE
United States, east of the Rocky Mountains; southern and central Canada

WINTER RANGE
United States, east of the Rocky Mountains

NORTHERN ORIOLE

Icterus polbula, Blackbird family (*ICTERIDAE*)

The northern oriole builds one of the most unusual nests of any North American bird. It weaves a hanging basket of grass, plant fibers, plant down, yarn, string, and spider webs.

PLUMAGE
Black head, back, wings, and tail; orange breast, underside, and bands on shoulders; white wing bars; female greenish-brown with duller underside and wing bars

BILL
Long, pointed, silver

FEET
Anisodactylous, silvery gray

LENGTH
About 7½" (19 cm)

RELATIVE SIZE
Between house sparrow and European starling

SONG
Sounds like a series of flutelike whistles

HABITAT
Woodlands and residential areas with mature deciduous trees

FOOD
Insects, spiders, some fruits, seeds; not much of a feeder bird, but will come for orange segments

BREEDING RANGE
United States except deep south; southern Canada

WINTER RANGE
South of the United States

BULLOCK'S ORIOLE

Icterus bullockii, Blackbird family (*ICTERIDAE*)

When it was first discovered that the northern oriole of the east and the Bullock's oriole of west bred, ornithologists combined the two into one species under the northern oriole moniker. Although they do interbreed, they still show preference for mates of their own kind. Consequently, the Bullock's oriole has been re-established as its own species.

PLUMAGE
Black head, neck, back, wings, and trail; orange face, underside, and outer tail feathers; white wing patches; females grayish upper, dull yellow underside, gray belly

BILL
Long, pointed, gray

FEET
Anisodactylous, gray

LENGTH
About 7" (18 cm)

RELATIVE SIZE
Between house sparrow and European starling

SONG
Sounds like a series of flutelike whistles

HABITAT
Woodlands and residential areas with mature trees

FOOD
Insects, spiders, some fruits, and seeds; not much of a feeder bird

BREEDING RANGE
Western United States, southwestern Canada

WINTER RANGE
Mexico, Central America

PURPLE FINCH

Carpodacus purpureus, Finch family (*FRINGILLIDAE*)

A flock of purple finches is an awesome eating machine. The birds will descend on a feeding area, dominate the feeders for hours on end, and consume huge quantities of available seed.

PLUMAGE
Dull red with gray-brown tint on wings and tail; female and young are more brownish

BILL
Short, conical, gray

FEET
Anisodactylous, gray-brown

LENGTH
About 6" (15 cm)

RELATIVE SIZE
House sparrow

SONG
Sounds like a warble, ending in a downward trill

HABITAT
Woodlands and residential areas with trees

FOOD
Seeds, fruit, and berries and some insects and spiders; at the feeder: prefers niger seeds

BREEDING RANGE
Northern United States, southern and central Canada

WINTER RANGE
United States except Great Plains

HOUSE FINCH

Carpodacus mexicanus, Finch family *(FRINGILLIDAE)*

The house finch is today one of the most widespread and common backyard birds in the northeastern United States. However, there was no population east of the Great Plains before the early 1940s when several New York City pet shops released birds they had been selling illegally.

PLUMAGE
Streaked gray-brown and buff with red head, breast, and rump; female similar but without red

BILL
Short, conical, gray

FEET
Anisodactylous, gray-brown

LENGTH
About 5" (12.5 cm)

RELATIVE SIZE
Between American goldfinch and house sparrow

SONG
Sounds like "zzree-zzree;" also "cheep"

HABITAT
Residential areas

FOOD
Seeds, fruits, berries; also insects and spiders when nesting; at the feeder: prefers sunflower and niger seed

BREEDING AND WINTER RANGE
Northeastern, mid-Atlantic, and western United States; southwestern Canada.

COMMON REDPOLL

Carduelis flammea, Finch family *(FRINGILLIDAE)*

Flocks of common redpolls will seep through patches of weeds in winter, knocking seeds from dried seedpods and flowers heads to the ground. As a group, they will land on the fallen seed to eat.

PLUMAGE
Streaked brown and buff with red cap; darker chin; rose breast

BILL
Short, sharp, silvery

FEET
Anisodactylous, dark gray

LENGTH
About 5½" (14 cm)

RELATIVE SIZE
Between American goldfinch and house sparrow

SONG
Series of soft twittering and rattling

HABITAT
Brushy areas, weedy areas, thickets

FOOD
Seeds, fruit, insects, spiders when nesting; at the feeder: prefers niger and oil-type sunflower seeds

BREEDING RANGE
Northern Canada, Alaska

WINTER RANGE
Northern United States, southern Canada

PINE SISKIN

Carduelis pinus, Finch family (*FRINGILLIDAE*)

The pine siskin is one of the northern finches that isn't generally seen at feeders in most of North American coniferous woodlands in summer; residential areas and deciduous woodlands in winters of irruption, until the native seed crop fails in the northern Canadian forests, forcing it south in large numbers.

PLUMAGE
Streaked gray, brown, and black with yellow patches on wings and tail

BILL
Short, conical, black

FEET
Anisodactylous, dark gray

LENGTH
About 4½" (11.5 cm)

RELATIVE SIZE
American goldfinch

SONG
Series of rasping chirps, twitters, and twirls; also "bzzzzt"

HABITAT
Woodlands, thickets, brushy areas

FOOD
Seeds, some insects, and spiders: at the feeder: prefers niger seed

BREEDING RANGE
Northern United States, Canada

WINTER RANGE
United States, Canadian Pacific coast

AMERICAN GOLDFINCH

Carduelis tristis, Finch family (*FRINGILLIDAE*)

For many years, it was believed the American goldfinch, one of the last species to nest in summer each year, waited for the down to develop on thistle flower heads before building its nest. That way, it could use the down to line its nest. More recently, it's been determined that it's the abundant food source of ripe thistle seed that actually is playing into the bird's timing.

PLUMAGE
Lemon yellow with black forehead, wings, and tail; white at tips of wings, tail, and rump; female is duller in color; in the fall, the male is also duller

BILL
Short, conical, orange

FEET
Anisodactylous, orange

LENGTH
About 4" (10 cm)

RELATIVE SIZE
The American goldfinch—at about 4" (10 cm) in length from beak to tail—is the standard of comparison for most backyard bird sizes

SONG
Succession of high-pitched twitters and trills; also makes a call that sounds like "per-chick-a-ree, per-chick-a-ree," usually while in flight

HABITAT
Brushy areas, thickets, weedy areas

FOOD
Seeds, insects, and spiders while nesting; at the feeder: prefers niger seed

BREEDING RANGE
Northern United States and southern Canada

WINTER RANGE
Same as breeding range, except not in Great Plains or Rocky Mountains

EVENING GROSBEAK

Coccothraustes vespertinus, Finch family (*FRINGILLIDAE*)

Some winters, large flocks of evening grosbeaks show up at backyard feeders in the United States. But other years, not one will be spotted. As with the other northern finches, it all depends on the success or failure of the natural seed crop in the northern forests. When the grosbeaks do come south, they are heavy-eating bullies at feeders.

PLUMAGE
Black head with yellow eyebrow; yellow shoulders and breast; black wings and tail with white patches; female similar but grayish

BILL
Large, conical, greenish-yellow

FEET
Anisodactylous, pink

LENGTH
About 8" (20 cm)

RELATIVE SIZE
Starling

SONG
Sounds like a series of brief and abrupt whistles

HABITAT
Northern coniferous woodlands in summer; residential areas and deciduous woodlands in winters

FOOD
Seeds, fruits; at the feeder: prefers sunflower seeds

BREEDING RANGE
New England and mountain regions of the western United States, south and central Canada

WINTER RANGE
Northern United States, southern Canada

House Sparrow

Passer domesticus, Sparrow family *(PASSERIDAE)*

The house sparrow, being an immigrant to North America, doesn't have its own natural niche, so it is lives in proximity to human development. Native to Asia, Europe, and Africa, the species was introduced to the United States in 1850 when a few pairs were released in New York City's Central Park.

PLUMAGE
Gray cheek, breast, sides, and belly; black and tan on wings and tail; red-brown cap; black throat; female and young are duller

BILL
Short, conical, tan or cream

FEET
Anisodactylous, gray

LENGTH
About 6" (15 cm)

RELATIVE SIZE
House sparrow

SONG
Sounds like a nonmusical series of chirps

HABITAT
Residential and agricultural areas

FOOD
Seeds, fruits, insects, and spiders; at the feeder: prefers cracked corn and sunflower seeds

BREEDING AND WINTER RANGE
United States, south and central Canada, Europe, Africa, and Asia

COOPER'S HAWK

Accipiter cooperii, Hawl family *(ACCIPITRIDAE)*

Backyard birdwatchers are finding that they've established a secondary feeder situation: Cooper's hawk—a specialist in taking smaller birds as prey—discover an abundant feeding station of songbirds that are attracted to feeders. It will continue to hunt that prey base until it no longer finds it beneficial. Birdwatchers can temporarily stop feeding the songbirds until they disburse enough to disinterest the Cooper's hawk, or they can add a bit more escape cover near feeders and accept the loss of some songbirds.

PLUMAGE
Blue-gray back, tail, and upper wings; white breast, belly, and under wings with thin reddish bars; black cap

BILL
Short, hooked, gray tipped with darker gray

FEET
Muscular, raptorial, with hooked yellowish talons

LENGTH
About 17" (43 cm)

RELATIVE SIZE
American crow

SONG
Sounds like a series of short, sharp "cherts" with a nasal tone

HABITAT
Mixed woodlands; agricultural, suburban, and rural areas with mature deciduous trees

FOOD
Birds, small mammals; at the feeder: prefers small birds

BREEDING RANGE
United States, southern Canada

WINTER RANGE
South of the United States

COMMON BACKYARD BIRD SPECIES

The bird descriptions that follow are arranged by families. This organization will make it easier to identify them using the size comparison and identity factors listed.

UNITED KINGDOM AND EUROPEAN BIRDS

The hedgerows, open fields, and parks of the United Kingdom and Northern Europe are home to an abundance of interesting bird species, which can be coaxed to set up housekeeping in backyards when the right feed and habitat plants are provided.

GREAT-SPOTTED WOODPECKER

Dendrocopos major, Woodpecker family *(PICIDAE)*

The song of the male great-spotted woodpecker is unlike that of most other backyard birds. It's a rapid drumming on the trunk or a large branch of a tree, about twenty strikes per second. The female, which will be maintaining her own territory at some distance from that of the male, will approach the source of the drumming, and a pair-bond good for two or three years may be formed.

PLUMAGE
Black and white above; off-white underside; bright red rump and back of head

BILL
Shorts, pointed, silver

FEET
Zygodactylous, gray

LENGTH
About 9" (23 cm)

RELATIVE SIZE
Between bullfinch and magpie

SONG
Drumming, but also has a loud call of "chitch"

HABITAT
Woodlands, parks, backyards with mature trees

FOOD
Insects, spiders, nuts, berries; at the feeder: prefers peanuts, suet

BREEDING AND WINTER RANGE
United Kingdom, except Ireland and Scotland; all but Northern Europe

WINTER WREN

Troglodytes troglodytes, Wren family (*TROGLODYTIDAE*)

The dull little wren is often missed as it flits through the densest undergrowth. It's more visible—but still easy to miss—as it hops along fences and walls. The tiny male maintains a large territory, which it fills in the spring with many nests tucked into cavities and on top of the old nests of other birds before commencing to sing to attract a mate. When a female accepts the invitation, she selects one of the nests and lines it with feathers. A male with prime territory may attract several females to his various nests.

PLUMAGE
Brown cap, nape, back, wings, and tail; grayish stripe over eye; black bars on wings; lighter underside

BILL
Long, pointed, orange

FEET
Anisodactylous, light brown

LENGTH
About 3 ½" (9 cm)

RELATIVE SIZE
Wren

SONG
Loud, high-pitched trilling

HABITAT
Undergrowth in parks, backyards, and woodlands

FOOD
Insects, spiders; at the feeder: prefers suet, mealworms, and tiny table scraps

BREEDING AND WINTER RANGE
United Kingdom, Europe

ROBIN

Erithacus rubecula, Old World Flycatcher family *(MUSCICAPIDAE)*

The robin has spread into the wooded, undergrowth-choked gardens and parks of the United Kingdom but has kept to its natural woodland habitat throughout most of Europe. In either setting, the bird is aggressively defensive of its territory throughout the year because of the vital food source of worms and insects that it eats in huge quantities.

PLUMAGE
Olive-brown head, back, and wings; tan tail; bright reddish-orange face and breast; buff underside

BILL
Short, pointed, black

FEET
Anisodactylous, reddish brown

LENGTH
About 5½" (14 cm)

RELATIVE SIZE
Between wren and bullfinch

SONG
Repeated "tseeeee" or "tic"

HABITAT
Woodlands, hedgerows, backyards with trees and shrubs

FOOD
Worms, insects, spider, berries; not much of a feeder bird

BREEDING RANGE
United Kingdom, all but northern Europe

WINTER RANGE
United Kingdom, southern half of Europe

DUNNOCK

Prunella modularis, Accentor family (*PRUNELLIDAE*)

Although the dunnock is a relatively shy and secluded species in continental Europe, in the United Kingdom, it has become a common backyard bird. Where it does occur, the males and females maintain separate but overlapping ranges. One male may mate with several of the females in territories intersecting his own; likewise, one female may consort with multiple males.

PLUMAGE
Gray crown with brown streaks; gray head, throat, and breast; brown wings streaked with gray; gray-brown rump

BILL
Long, pointed, black

FEET
Anisodactylous, pink

LENGTH
About 5½" (14 cm)

RELATIVE SIZE
Between wren and bullfinch

SONG
Repeated high-pitched warbling jingle

HABITAT
Mixed woodland, grasslands with shrubs, parks, backyards

FOOD
Insects, spiders, seeds; at the feeder: prefers sunflower seeds, suet

BREEDING RANGE
United Kingdom, all but northern Europe

WINTER RANGE
United Kingdom, southern Europe

European Blackbird

Turdus merula, Thrush family (*TURDIDAE*)

A highly adaptable species, the blackbird has spread into nearly every habitat throughout the United Kingdom and southern Europe, so that today it is the most common bird species. It is not highly selective about locating its nest of grasses, weed stems, and litter and can produce as many as four clutches every year. It also will eat just about anything it finds.

PLUMAGE
Jet black overall; yellow eye ring and bill

BILL
Long, pointed, bright yellow

FEET
Anisodactylous, dark brown

LENGTH
About 9"–10" (23–24.5 cm)

RELATIVE SIZE
Between bullfinch and magpie

SONG
Loud, rising and falling warble that trails off at the end

HABITAT
Nearly everywhere

FOOD
Worms, insects, fruit, berries, seeds; at the feeder: prefers sunflower seeds, suet, old fruit, and table scraps

BREEDING RANGE
United Kingdom, Europe

WINTER RANGE
United Kingdom, all but northern Europe

SONG THRUSH

Turdus philomelos, Thrush family (*TURDIDAE*)

The song thrush has been disappearing from many backyards and agricultural areas, thought to be largely the result of loss of prime hedgerow habitat and the accompanying food base. Worms are an important part of that food base, although the song thrush is noted for its ability to break open the shell of a snail and dig out the soft meat from inside.

PLUMAGE
Brown head, back, shoulders, and wings; buff to white underside, heavily speckled with black and brown spots

BILL
Long, pointed, black

FEET
Anisodactylous, reddish-brown

LENGTH
About 9" (23 cm)

RELATIVE SIZE
Between bullfinch and magpie

SONG
Flutelike, musical series of notes, repeated three or four times

HABITAT
Edges of woodlands, parks, backyards, and fields

FOOD
Worms, insects, fruit, snails; at the feeder: prefers bits of apple, suet, table scraps

BREEDING AND WINTER RANGE
United Kingdom, southwestern Europe

GOLDCREST

Regulus regulus, Kinglet family *(SYLVIIDAE)*

The goldcrest is the smallest bird in Europe, often difficult to spot but easy to locate by its distinctive song. There have even been reports of individuals of this species becoming trapped in spider webs.

PLUMAGE
Olive-green cap and back; bright yellow crest outlined in black; greenish buff underside; dark gray wings with two bands of black and white

BILL
Short, pointed, black

FEET
Anisodactylous, pink

LENGTH
About 3½" (9 cm)

RELATIVE SIZE
Wren

SONG
Sounds like "tweedly-tweedly-tweedly-tweedly"

HABITAT
Coniferous woodlands, hedgerows, parks, and backyards with coniferous trees

FOOD
Insects and spiders; not much of a feeder bird

BREEDING RANGE
United Kingdom, all but northern Europe

WINTER RANGE
United Kingdom, central Europe

COAL TIT

Parus ater, Titmouse family *(PARIDAE)*

The coal tit is a natural hoarder, storing seeds plucked from conifer cones and feeders every chance it gets throughout the fall. It is one of the most active backyard birds, flitting to the feeder to grab a seed and then back into the branches of a nearby conifer to either eat the kernel inside or store the whole seed.

PLUMAGE
Black head with white cheek patches and nape of neck; gray back; darker gray wings with white bands; buff underside

BILL
Short, pointed, black

FEET
Anisodactylous, dark gray

LENGTH
About 4½" (11.5 cm)

RELATIVE SIZE
Between wren and bullfinch

SONG
Repeated, high-pitched "seetoooee"

HABITAT
Coniferous and mixed woodlands, parks, and backyards with conifers

FOOD
Insects, spiders, seeds, nuts; at the feeder: prefers sunflower seeds, suet

BREEDING AND WINTER RANGE
United Kingdom, all except northern Europe and coastal Italy

BLUE TIT

Parus caeruleus, Titmouse family *(PARIDAE)*

Blue tits are among the most exploratory and inventive of backyard birds, always on the search for new ways to exploit food sources, regardless of the acrobatics those new methods might require. The little bird is also lightweight and agile, allowing it to approach a new method from whatever angle might be necessary. The species also is remarkably unafraid of humans, allowing for full use of our backyards.

PLUMAGE
Bright blue cap; white face with black eye-line and chin; bright blue wings with single band of white; greenish blue back; bright blue tail; yellowish underside

BILL
Short, conical, black

FEET
Anisodactylous, silver

LENGTH
About 4¹⁄₂" (11.5 cm)

RELATIVE SIZE
Between wren and bullfinch

SONG
Sounds like "tsee-tsee-tsu-tu-tu-tu-tu"

HABITAT
Deciduous woodlands, gardens, and parks with trees

FOOD
Insects, spiders, fruit, seeds; at the feeder: prefers bits of fruit, suet, sunflower seeds, shelled peanuts, and table scraps

BREEDING AND WINTER RANGE
United Kingdom, all but northern Europe

MAGPIE

Pica pica, Crow family (*CORVIDAE*)

The magpie is another opportunistic species that has thrived through an association with human-dominated landscapes. Taking advantage of roadkill, trash, and backyard feeders, the species has expanded its range. Persecution from gamekeepers, trying to lessen the magpie's impact on the nests, eggs, and nestlings of other bird species, has lessened in recent years, also boosting the magpie's range spread.

PLUMAGE
Black head, breast, back, and tail; white shoulder and belly; white wing tips with black tips

BILL
Strong, pointed, black

FEET
Anisodactylous, black

LENGTH
About 18" (45.5 cm)

RELATIVE SIZE
Magpie

SONG
Sounds like "chak-chak-chak-chak"

HABITAT
Deciduous woodlands, parks, and backyards with trees, farmlands with trees

FOOD
Nearly anything edible; at the feeder: prefers table scraps, suet, peanuts in shell

BREEDING AND WINTER RANGE
All but northern United Kingdom, all but northern Europe

Jackdaw

Corvus monedula, Crow family *(CORVIDAE)*

The jackdaw is a highly sociable bird, traveling and nesting in flocks made up of mated pairs, which remain faithful to one another. Each pair shares nesting duties, with the exception of incubating the eggs, which is the duty of the female alone. The nest, in whatever cavity or crevice can be found, is a large mass of sticks mixed with everything from hair to old rags to street litter and mud.

PLUMAGE
Mostly black with a purplish sheen; gray on the cheeks and neck

BILL
Large, conical, black

FEET
Anisodactylous, black

LENGTH
About 13" (33 cm)

RELATIVE SIZE
Between bullfinch and magpie

SONG
Varying medley of notes, including several well-spaced "tchak" calls

HABITAT
Woodlands, farmlands, towns, parks

FOOD
Insects, nuts, fruits, berries, eggs of other birds; at the feeder: prefers suet and table scraps

BREEDING AND WINTER RANGE
United Kingdom, all but northern Europe

EUROPEAN STARLING

Sturnus vulgaris, Starling family (*STURNIDAE*)

Being a natural part of the ecosystem in Europe, the starling is a better fit with other birds than it has become in North America, where their import threatens many native cavity-nesting birds. Even in Europe, however, the male starling is a staunch defender of the territory around his nesting cavity, which often is also his territory throughout the year.

PLUMAGE
Black with many tiny, white speckles and an overall sheen of green to purple, depending on the light

BILL
Long, pointed, yellow

FEET
Anisodactylous, reddish

LENGTH
About 8" (20 cm)

RELATIVE SIZE
Between bullfinch and magpie

SONG
Electrical combination of squeaks and rattles

HABITAT
Open, grassy areas

FOOD
Worms, grubs, insects, wide range of plant material; at the feeder: prefers suet, shelled peanuts, sunflower seeds, and table scraps

BREEDING AND WINTER RANGE
United Kingdom, southwestern Europe

CHAFFINCH

Fringilla coelebs, Finch family *(FRINGILLIDAE)*

The chaffinch has a diverse vocal repertoire, with many localized dialects. To begin the mating season, the male alights to one of his territory's singing posts—usually prominent branches near the tops of trees—and loudly proclaims his territorial claim and his desire for a mate. When a pair bonds, the male's territory becomes both their nesting area and their feeding area.

PLUMAGE
Blue-gray head with pinkish cheek and around the eye, breast and belly; brown back; olive rump, black wings with white bars; white tail edges

BILL
Short, conical, yellow

FEET
Anisodactylous, gray

LENGTH
About 6" (15 cm)

RELATIVE SIZE
Bullfinch

SONG
Sounds like "chip-chip-chip-chiwee-chiwee-tissichooee"

HABITAT
Woodlands, parks, backyards, fields

FOOD
Seeds, fruits, insects; at the feeder

BREEDING RANGE
United Kingdom, Europe

WINTER RANGE
United Kingdom, southern Europe

GREENFINCH

Carduelis chloris, Finch family (*FRINGILLIDAE*)

The greenfinch is a common backyard bird wherever feeders are provided. A backyard with coniferous trees is all the more attractive to this species, which prefers the evergreens for its small colony of nests, made of twigs, grasses, and moss and lined with hair and rootlets. The females of the colony often begin building new nests before the first brood has been fledged, leaving the final familial duties to the males.

PLUMAGE
Greenish overall, with a yellowish tint on the underside; yellow edges on the wings and tail

BILL
Short, conical, pink

FEET
Anisodactylous, pink

LENGTH
About 6" (15 cm)

RELATIVE SIZE
Bullfinch

SONG
Serious of varying notes, ending in a loud wheeze

HABITAT
Edges of parks, backyards, orchards, and woodlands

FOOD
Seeds, buds, berries, insects; at the feeder: prefers sunflower seeds, shelled peanuts

BREEDING AND WINTER RANGE
United Kingdom, all but northern Europe

SISKIN

Carduelis spinus, Finch family *(FRINGILLIDAE)*

The siskin population has expanded its range into the backyards of the United Kingdom and Europe over the past half century in response to the residential landscape planting of conifers, the seeds of which are a primary food source for the bird and the branches of which are the preferred nesting site.

PLUMAGE
Yellowish-green cheeks, neck, back, and breast; black cap and wings; white underside

BILL
Short, conical, silver

FEET
Pinkish gray

LENGTH
About 4½" (11.5 cm)

RELATIVE SIZE
Between wren and bullfinch

SONG
Melodious twittering, ending in a loud wheeze

HABITAT
Coniferous and mixed woodlands

FOOD
Seeds, buds, berries, insects; at the feeder: prefers peanuts, sunflower seeds, suet

BREEDING AND WINTER RANGE
United Kingdom, all but northern Europe

BULLFINCH

Pyrrhula pyrrhula, Finch family *(FRINGILLIDAE)*

A highly secretive bird, the bullfinch tends to keep to thick undergrowth. Its whistling call is often the best clue to its presence. The male of the pair selects the nesting site in the dense foliage; the female builds the nest of twigs lined with rootlets. Both parents participate in rearing the young. They also tend to stay together throughout the year.

PLUMAGE
Black head, flight feathers, and tail; orange to pink underside; gray shoulders; white rump

BILL
Short, conical, black

FEET
Anisodactylous, dark gray-brown

LENGTH
About 6" (15 cm)

RELATIVE SIZE
Bullfinch

SONG
Warbling whistle, "deu-deu"

HABITAT
Brushy areas, thickets, hedgerows

FOOD
Seeds, fruit tree buds; at the feeder: prefers sunflower seeds, shelled peanuts

BREEDING AND WINTER RANGE
United Kingdom, western Europe

REED BUNTING

Emberiza schoeniclus, Sparrow family *(EMBERIZIDAE)*

The loss of wetlands has been hard on the reed bunting, but the small bird has responded by occupying drier areas that it historically occupied, such as grain fields, areas around ponds, and conifer plantations. The species still needs low-lying shrubs or tall clumps of grass for nesting.

PLUMAGE
Brown, streaked with black back, wings, and tail; black head with small white cheek patch; grayish-white collar and underside

BILL
Short, conical, tan

FEET
Anisodactylous, brown

LENGTH
About 6" (15 cm)

RELATIVE SIZE
Bullfinch

SONG
Sounds like "zip-zip-zip-zittityk," again and again

HABITAT
Wetlands, farmlands, hedgerows

FOOD
Insects, snails, seeds; at the feeder: prefers sunflower seeds, shelled peanuts

BREEDING RANGE
United Kingdom, southwestern Europe

WINTER RANGE
United Kingdom, Europe

6

BIRD STUDY

EXPANDING LIFE AS A BIRDWATCHER

There comes a time when it is no longer enough for a birder to be able to attract birds into the backyard for close-up observation, identify the different species on sight, and even know the bird from its song alone. It's time to raise the bar and enter the stage of full-on bird study.

All aspects of the avian life are now open for exploration from behavior to physiology. More specialized reading, even scientific publications, begins occupying a corner of the desk. Advanced nature-center, or even college courses, increasingly find their way onto the schedule.

While it's beyond the capabilities of this book to cover any of the topics in-depth, in this chapter you will find some of the possibilities for your new, deeper investigation of birds: the class, Aves, in the subphylum, Vertebrata, in the phylum, Chordata, and in the kingdom, Animalia.

ALL-SEASON TIP

Reports of rare birds being spotted generally attract large numbers of birdwatchers, each wanting to add the check mark for that bird to their life list (a list of bird species sighted in a lifetime). At high-stress times of the year, such as during migration, the depth of winter, and the mating/nesting season, such announcements can pose real dangers to these birds. Before making such information widely known, assess how much potential there is for encroaching birders to disturb the unusual birds, the habitat, landowners, and other humans in the vicinity.

Birding is the type of hobby that never grows stale because there are always new levels to which the birder can advance and new areas of inquiry and study presenting themselves.

ANATOMY AND PHYSIOLOGY

To think about bird physiology is to explore a foreign world. Sure, birds are warm-blooded like mammals; their normal body temperature is about 104°F (40°C). They have two eyes, two ears, (although they are not usually visible) and two nostrils (although most have little or no sense of smell). But, birds have followed a different evolutionary path to gain the ability to fly, making a great many anatomical concessions along the way.

Weight Adaptations

Weight is a central concern when trying to lift any object off the ground. Birds have attacked that problem evolutionarily by giving up heavy teeth and large, weighty jaw bones necessitated by teeth. They've given up mass in their skull bones. The bony, muscular tail—so prominent in some ground-dwelling mammals—has been replaced by a rump of light and maneuverable feathers.

The primary bones in a bird's leg are hollow, relying on ligament rather than bone mass for their internal strength, but that is not part of their weight-reduction system. Often, the leg bones of a bird are heavier than the leg bones of similarly sized mammals.

Importance of Lift

A source of lift is the second major necessity for flight. Birds flap wings to produce lift which requires relatively enormous muscles attached quite solidly to their skeleton. The enlarged sternum of birds,—missing in some flightless species—the fusing of some groups of vertebrae,

and additional lateral growth in the ribs have accommodated this need.

A bird's body, at least in those species that fly, is generally compact and compressed in comparison to many other vertebrates. The legs and wings operate closer to the bird's center of gravity, improving their efficiency and balance.

All avian bodies follow the same basic plan, although there are huge variations evolved for different lifestyles. Geese have more vertebrae in their necks than sparrows to allow them to better utilize their aquatic habitat, including pond bottoms and the like. Most flightless birds have left the enlarged sternum in their evolutionary dust, except the penguin, which basically flies through the water and still needs strong wing muscles to propel itself.

Toe, Claw, and Bill Shape and Function

Toe arrangement, claw shape and size, and bill size and shape, are additional, highly evolved parts of bird anatomy and reveal incredible amounts of information about a species' life.

Most of our backyard songbirds are perching birds. They have a foot configuration known as anisodactyl that is perfect for grasping perches: long, independent, flexible toes, three pointing forward and one backwards. Woodpeckers have two toes pointing forward and two backwards, a configuration known as zygodactyls, which is perfect for climbing the sides of tree trunks. Waterbirds, such as geese and ducks, have palmate feet, meaning they have webbing between their toes to propel them through the

Birds' feet have three basic shapes, depending on the terrain the various species travels. Perching birds have three toes pointing forward and one toe pointing backward in an arrangement called anisodactyl. Wood-peckers have two toes pointing forward and two to the back, in a configuration called zygodactyl, which makes it possible for them to climb trees. Waterbirds have webbed feet, called palmate, to propel them through water.

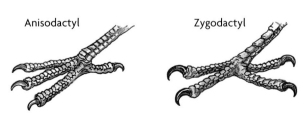

Anisodactyl   Zygodactyl

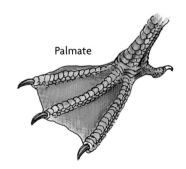

Palmate

Hummingbirds regularly consume more than half their weight in sweet flower nectar (or nectar from feeders) every day to fuel their high-energy style of flight, burning energy at a rate equivalent to a man running 9 miles (14.5 km) per hour.

water. The toes of wading birds are relatively long and flat to spread the weight of the bird out over a maximum area and effectively move through and beside water. Raptors, such as hawks and owls, have muscular, inward-curving toes equipped with large claws called talons for snatching and killing their prey.

Adaptive evolution has also supplied birds with a wide array of food-gathering tools to fit the various niches of the ecosystem at the opposite end of their bodies. Beaks—ranging from short and stout to long and slender to razor sharp and hooked—have all adapted to make the best use of available foods. For more on beak shape and eating habits, see page 15.

Flight

The bottom of a bird's wing is flat. The top is arched. As the bird takes flight, air passes over both surfaces of the wing, but the air is forced to travel faster over the top of the wing in order to cover the longer distance of the arched surface in the same amount of time as the air that passes beneath the flat underside of the wing. That causes a difference in air pressure, resulting in a lift beneath the wing. However, the airflow also pushes back against the wing in a force called drag that the bird must overcome by flapping the wing.

Flapping is a high-energy-consumption activity, best suited for flying short distances. Lift and propulsion are created on the downward stroke. Drag is generated on the upward stroke, which the bird reduces by folding the wing as it moves upward.

Gliding is the form of flight birds use in longer distance travel. Wings stretched out stiffly act as airfoils, creating low pressure above and higher pressure below. The difference again results in lift.

To turn in midair, a bird can change the tilt of one of its wings in the direction it wants to fly, flap one wing faster than the other, and use the tail to maneuver.

ALL-SEASON TIP

Any time of year is the right time to begin a permanent record of your bird sightings. Each day that you don't have such a "life list" is another day worth of sightings lost forever. Use a permanent notebook or journal, with a strong binding and quality paper for pages, to make your record a long-lived volume.

POPULATION DYNAMICS

A population is the number of individuals of a species in a defined area, kept in check by limiting factors of all the elements of that species' niche: food, water, shelter from enemies and the elements of weather, a safe and secure place to reproduce and rear young, and space.

In the natural world, no population exists independent of other populations—animal and plant—in a given ecosystem. It's like a jigsaw puzzle with all the pieces depending upon others to maintain the whole.

A complex community of plants and animals in a region and a climate is called a biome. Some of biomes on Earth are grassland, temperate deciduous forest, coniferous forest, chaparral or scrub, wetlands, freshwater marsh, ponds, lake, rivers, streams, desert, tundra, taiga, mountain alpine, various oceanic zones, and many more.

Within their populations, communities, and biomes, all living things build and use symbiotic relationships with other species. In mutualistic symbiosis, both species benefit; commensal symbiosis, one species benefits and the other sees no impact; parasitic symbiosis, one species benefits and the other is harmed as a result; and mimicry, one species imitates the other to gain the benefits of being recognized as the latter.

BIODIVERSITY AND CONSERVATION

Biodiversity is the variety of plants, animals, and microorganisms—their genes, and the ecosystems of which they are a part. In the more modern context, biodiversity is the fight to preserve as much of that variety as possible.

Global Concern

More and more humans are becoming concerned about our planet's declining biodiversity—which is still debated by some scientists and policy-makers—because everything we need to survive is based on biodiversity—goods, medicine, clothing, and more. Endangered species may hold yet-to-be discovered medicines. And, after all, it's the diversity of the Earth's biological community that performs air and water purification, climate regulation, oxygen generation, and more.

Some scientists, like Denis Saunders of Australia's Commonwealth Scientific and Industrial Research Organization, believe 70,000 species become extinct every year because of the demands of an out-of-control human population and that half of all species will be lost in the twenty-first century. He sees human activity as causing a crisis of biodiversity, the largest mass extinction in 65 million years.

The full complexity of the natural world is something none of us may ever achieve with our backyard habitat. Although, the more diversity we provide, the closer we come to that goal.

Bird Organizations

**AMERICAN ASSOCIATION
OF WILDLIFE VETERINARIANS**
c/o Dr. Kristin Mansfield, Secretary
AAWV
Washington Dept. of Fish and Wildlife
8702 N. Division Street
Spokane, WA 99218 USA
www.aawv.net/

BIRDLIFE INTERNATIONAL
Wellbrook Court, Girton Road
Cambridge CB3 0NA United Kingdom
44.(0).1223.277318
birdlife@birdlife.org

BIRD SOURCE
www.birdsource.org

BIRD STUDIES CANADA
P.O. Box 6227
Sackville NB E4L 1G6, Canada
506.364.5025
colin.carroll@ec.gc.ca

BIRD WATCH IRELAND
Ruttledge House
8 Longford Place, Monkstown, Co.
Dublin, Ireland
www.birdwatchireland.ie

CATS INDOORS! CAMPAIGN
American Bird Conservancy
1731 Connecticut Ave, NW
Washington, DC 20009 USA
202.234.7181
www.abcbirds.org/cats/

COOPER ORNITHOLOGICAL SOCIETY
c/o Bonnie S. Bowen
124 Science Hall II, Iowa State University
Ames, IA 50011 USA
254.399.9636
www.cooper.org/

EUROBIRDING
www.eurobirding.com

FAT BIRDER
www.fatbirder.com

ARTHUR GROSSET
www.arthurgrosset.com

**INTERNATIONAL ASSOCIATION OF
FISH AND WILDLIFE AGENCIES**
444 North Capitol Street, NW, Suite 725
Washington, DC 20001 USA
202.624.7890
www.iafwa.org/

LINCOLNSHIRE WILDLIFE TRUST
Banovallum House
Manor House Street, Homcastle
Lincolnshire, LN9 5HF United Kingdom
44 (0) 0150.752.6667
www.lincstrust.org.uk

LIGUE POUR LA PROTECION DES OISEAUX
www.lpo.fr

**NATIONAL ASSOCIATION OF STATE PUBLIC
HEALTH VETERINARIANS, INC.**
P.O. 13528
Baltimore, MD 21203 USA

NATIONAL AUDUBON SOCIETY
700 Broadway
New York, NY 10003-9562 USA
212.979.3000
audubonaction@audubon.org

NATIONAL WILDLIFE FEDERATION
Backyard Habitat Program
P.O. Box 1583
Merrifield, VA, 22116-1583 USA
800.822.9919
www.nwf.org/

NATURE CANADA
606-1 Nicholas Street
Ottawa ON K1N 7B7 Canada
800.267.4088
info@naturecanada.ca.

NATURSCHUTZBUND
Deutschland
NABU@NABU.de
www.nabu.de

**THE ROYAL SOCIETY FOR
THE PROTECTION OF BIRDS**
The Lodge
Sandy Bedfordshire SG19 2DL, United Kingdom
44.(0).1767.680551
www.rspb.org.uk

SCOTTISH ORNITHOLOGISTS' CLUB
21 Regent Terrace
Edinburgh EH7 5BT, United Kingdom
www.the-soc.org.uk

SOCIEDADE PORTUGUESA PARA
O ESTUDO DAS AVES
www.seo.org

SWEDISH ORNITHOLOGICAL SOCIETY
www.sofnet.org

SVS-BIRDLIFE SUISSE
svs@birdlife.ch
www.birdlife.ch

WELSH ORNITHOLOGICAL SOCIETY
196 Chester Road
Hartford
Northwich, Cheshire, CW8 1LG, United Kingdom
www.bto.org/

THE WILDFOWL & WETLANDS TRUST (WWT)
Slimbridge,
Gloucestershire, GL2 7BT
United Kingdom
www.wwt.org.uk

THE WILDLIFE TRUSTS
The Kiln, Waterside
Mather Road, Newark
Nottinghamshire, NG24 1WT, United Kingdom
www.wildlifetrusts.org

Quality Bird Seeds and Mixes

C J WILD BIRD FOODS LTD.
The Rea, Upton Magna
Shrewsbury SY4 4UR, United Kingdom
www.birdfood.co.uk

HAITH'S
65 Park Street
Cleethorpes
Lincolnshire DN35 7NF, United Kingdom
www.haiths.com

KAYTEE PRODUCTS, INC.
521 Clay Street,
P.O. Box 230,
Chilton, WI 53014 USA
www.kaytee.com

MAINE WILD BIRD FOOD COMPANY
11 Bangor Mall Blvd., Box 342,
Bangor, ME 04401 USA
www.mainebirdfood.com

WILD BIRDS FOREVER
27214 Highway 189, P.O. Box 4904
Blue Jay, CA 92317-4909 USA
www.birdsforever.com

Bird Feeders, Houses, Baths, and more

A BIRD'S WORLD.COM
www.abirdsworld.com

CHARLESTON GARDENS
650 King Street
Charleston, NC 29403 USA
843.722.7460
www.charlestongardens.com

DROLL YANKEES
27 Mill Road
Foster, RI 02825 USA
www.drollyankees.com

DUNCRAFT
102 Fisherville Road
Concord, NH 03303 USA
www.duncraft.com

HEATH MFG. CO.
140 Mill Street
Coopersville, MI 49404 USA
www.heathmfg.com

LOOKER PRODUCTS INC.
1017 North State Rt. 1
P.O. Box 29
Milford, IL 60953 USA
www.lookerinc.com

S&K MANUFACTURING
1001 Liberty Industrial Drive
O'Fallon, MO 63366 USA
www.sk-mfg.com

WILD BIRDS UNLIMITED, INC.
11711 N. College Ave.
Suite 146
Carmel, IN 46032 USA
www.wbu.com

Birding Magazines

AUDUBON MAGAZINE
National Audubon Society
700 Broadway
New York, NY 10003 USA

THE AUK
The American Ornithologists' Union
c/o Division of Birds MRC 116
National Museum of Natural History
Washington, DC 20560 USA

BBC WILDLIFE
P.O. Box 279
Sittingbourne,
Kent ME9 8DF, United Kingdom

BIRDWATCH
Warners, West Street
Bourne
Lincolnshire PE10 9PH, United Kingdom
www.birdwatch.co.uk

BIRD WATCHER'S DIGEST
P.O. Box 110
Marietta, OH 45750 USA

BIRD WATCHING
Emap, Bretton Court
Bretton
Peterborough PE3 8DZ United Kingdom

BIRDING
American Birding Association (ABA)
P.O. Box 6599
Colorado Springs, CO 80934 USA

BRITISH BIRDS
The Banks
Mountfield, Robertsbridge
East Sussex TN32 5JY, United Kingdom

THE CONDOR
Cooper Ornithological Society
810 East 10th St.
Lawrence, KS 66044 USA

LIVING BIRD
Cornell Laboratory of Ornithology
159 Sapsucker Woods Rd.
Ithaca, NY 14850 USA

WILDBIRD
P.O. Box 52898
Boulder, CO 80322 USA

THE WILSON BULLETIN
Wilson Ornithological Society
The Josselyn Van Tyne Memorial Library
Museum of Zoology, University of Michigan
Ann Arbor, MI 48109-1079 USA

WORLD BIRDWATCH
BirdLife International
Wellbrook Court, Girton Road,
Cambridge CB3 0NA United Kingdom

Birding Books

Beddard, Roy
THE GARDEN BIRD YEAR
New Holland Publishers, 2001

Cannon, Andrew
THE GARDEN BIRD WATCH HANDBOOK
British Trust for Ornithology, 2000

Garisto, Leslie
THE NEW BIRDHOUSE BOOK
Quarry Books, 2004

Golley, Mark, Moss, Stephen, and Daly, David
THE COMPLETE GARDEN BIRD BOOK
New Holland Publishers, 2001

Hammond, Nicholas, series editor
THE WILDLIFE TRUSTS GUIDE TO BIRDS
New Holland Publishers, 2002

Moss, Stephen
A BIRDWATCHER'S GUIDE: HOW TO BIRDWATCH
New Holland Publishers, 2003

Moss, Stephen and Cottridge, David
ATTRACTING BIRDS TO YOUR GARDEN
New Holland Publishers, 2000

Oddie, Bill
**BILL ODDIE'S INTRODUCTION
TO BIRDWATCHING**
New Holland Publishers, 2002

Soper, Tony
THE BIRD TABLE BOOK
David and Charles, 1992

GLOSSARY

ANISODACTYL: feet having three toes facing forward and one facing back

BILL: beak

BIRDER: birdwatcher, bird enthusiast

BREAST: front part of a bird's chest

CAP: top of the crown

COVERTS: small feathers covering the bases of other, usually larger, feathers

CREST: a tuft of elongated feathers on the bird's crown

CROWN: the uppermost surface of the head

EYE RING: the fleshy, or feathered ring, around the eye

EYE STRIPE: a stripe running horizontally from the base of the bill through the eye

FIELD GUIDE: a book with pictures of the birds and tips for finding and identifying them.

FLIGHT FEATHERS: long feathers of the wing and tail used for flight.

LORE: the area between the base of the bill and eye

MANDIBLE: one of the two parts (upper and lower) of a bird's bill

MANTLE: the back and the upper wing surfaces

NAPE: the back of the head and the hindneck

PALMATE: feet with webbing

RAPTOR: predatory, flesh-eating bird, including hawks, falcons, eagles, owls, ospreys, and vultures

RUMP: the lower back, just above the tail

ZYGODACTYL: feet with two toes facing forward and two facing back

BIBLIOGRAPHY

The Audubon Backyard Birdwatcher: Birdfeeders and *Bird Gardens* by Robert Burton, Stephen W. Bird Garden Kress, National Audubon Society, 1998, Thunder Bay Press.

The Backyard Bird Feeder's Bible: The A-to-Z Guide To Feeders, Seed Mixes, Projects and Treats by Sally Roth, 2000, Rodale Books.

The Birder's Handbook: A Field Guide to the Natural History of North American Birds by Paul Ehrlich, David S. Dobkin, and Darryl Wheye, 1998, Fireside.

A Field Guide to the Birds of Eastern and Central North America, Fifth Edition, by Roger Tory Peterson, 2002, Houghton Mifflin.

A Field Guide to Western Birds : A Completely New Guide to Field Marks of All Species Found in North America West of the 100th Meridian and North of Mexico (Peterson Field Guide Series) by Roger Tory Peterson, 1998, Houghton Mifflin.

National Geographic Field Guide to the Birds of North America, Fourth Edition, 2002, National Geographic Society.

The Sibley Field Guide to Birds of Eastern North America by David Allen Sibley, 2003, Knopf.

The Sibley Field Guide to Birds of Western North America by David Allen Sibley, 2003, Knopf.

The Sibley Guide to Bird Life and Behavior by David Allen Sibley, 2001, Knopf.

Stokes Guide to Bird Behavior, Volume 1, by Donald and Lillian Stokes, 1983, Little, Brown.

INDEX *(Italic page number denotes illustration.)*

PHOTOGRAPHER CREDITS

All photography by Maslowski Productions with the exception of the following:

Courtesy of Charleston Gardens
www.charlestongardens.com, 6 (top, left); 42; 67

Arthur Grosset
www.arthurgrosset.com, 2; 6 (top, right); 115; 138-157

Marcus H. Schneck
19 (right); 34 (right); 38; 39; 41; 56; 75; 77; 127; 131

Courtesy of Wild Birds Unlimited
www.wbu.com, 6 (bottom); 7 (top); 22; 23; 24; 34 (left); 35; 86; 99; 135; 161

All illustrations by Judy Love with the exception of page 58, Courtesy of Keith Davitt, Landscape Architect/www.gardenviews.com

Projects on the following pages excerpted from *The New Birdhouse Book*, © 2004 Quarry Books, 30; 32; 48; 50; 52

ABOUT THE AUTHOR

Marcus H. Schneck is the outdoor and nature editor at the *Patriot-News* in Harrisburg, Pennsylvania, editor of the outdoor and travel monthly magazine *Destinations*, and is a regular contributor to a range of outdoor, travel, nature, and general-interest magazines. He has written more than two dozen books on subjects including backyard birds, nature and the outdoors, travel, pets, and gardening. He lives and gardens to attract birds in historic Berks County, Pennsylvania.